Dimensions of the Enneagram:

Triad, Tradition, Transformation

by Thomas Garrett Isham

published by
The Lion and The Bee
Marshall, Michigan

ISBN: 0-923568-56-5

Cover illustration is from the frontispiece of the *Arithmologia* of Athanasius Kircher, published in Rome in 1665. Redrawn by Bruce Worden.

Scripture taken from the HOLY BIBLE, NEW INTERNATIONAL VERSION®. Copyright© 1973, 1978, 1984 by International Bible Society. Used by permission of Zondervan Publishing House. All rights reserved.

For Further Information, Please Contact:

The Lion and The Bee

P.O. Box 504

Marshall, MI 49068

Library of Congress Cataloging-in-Publication Data

Isham, Thomas Garrett, 1948-
Dimensions of the enneagram : triad, tradition, transformation
/ by
Thomas Garrett Isham.
p. cm.
Includes bibliographical references and index.
ISBN 0-923568-56-5
1. Enneagram. 2. Spiritual life. 3. Bible—Psychology. I. Title.
BL627.57.I84 2004
155.2'6—dc22
2003026615

Manufactured in the United States of America

In memory of Garrett Nelson Isham, father and friend

"Everything in this world we see is related to another world we do not see...we do indeed live
in a system of invisible things visibly manifested."
—Joseph de Maistre

Contents

Foreword

*"When the twofold law of human nature is annulled
and man's two poles are merged, he will be ONE, for,
being no longer torn by inner conflict,
how could the idea of duality occur to him?"*
—Joseph de Maistre

The Enneagram of Psychological Types is lively and active, able to pierce the division between soul and spirit, ego and essence. It penetrates the hidden self and bears practical issue. The results unburden the soul, heighten awareness, shape a paradigm for purposeful—and joyful—living. The Enneagram seeks to know what it is that makes people think and act the way they do; it explores the deepest wellsprings of their behavior, it provides deep and satisfying —and *true*—answers.

The book in hand, reflecting upon the Enneagram through a three-fold mirror of *Triad, Tradition and Transformation,* aims to explore:

- The "esoterist" or "esotericist" trends that underpin the system and its practical and theoretical wisdom.

- The "tripartite anthropology" of human nature in the context of Christian tradition and Enneagram theory.

- The psychological types and their traits, as enriched by the inclusion of sources from the distant to the recent past.

In regard to the first, there is an attempt to locate the Enneagram and its predecessors—and the religious and wisdom traditions they have influenced—within the stream of esoterist thought. This "form" of thought, for such it is, mines a rich vein of speculation and inner illumination. The Enneagram belongs to this tradition.

As to the second, the model of the "tripartite anthropology of man" is put forward as key to apprehending both the Enneagram and vital aspects of human nature.

Third, the nine types are enriched by material ancient and modern culled from the insights of perceptive, wise and—sometimes—holy men. These students of the psyche represent various schools and traditions and perspectives, all the better to illumine the subtle workings of the soul in all its complexity.

The heart of the book is aimed at the seeker of inner wisdom, at the one who would delve deeply into the richness of the manifold psyche, at the one who would explore the dark shadows and narrow constrictions of the ego—all with an eye to transcending the prison house of duality. Such a one is the one who will learn of the descent and ascent, the scattering and gathering, of the soul. Such a one is the one who will learn to integrate the scattered elements of distracted living into a more harmonious whole.

In addition, there is an attempt to fix the place of the Enneagram and its antecedents in the historic stream of Western wisdom, as this wisdom appears in Revelation and Reason, by way of Hebraic and Greek modes of understanding. This is a wisdom old yet new, dormant yet ready to be reawakened. It need but be rescued from the dust of neglect, brushed off, and brought forth into the sunlight, once again to take its place in the manners, mores and morals of human living.

1

The Interior Look

"Ibn 'Arabi mentions...that distress is to be welcomed as it incites the soul to move forward."
—Titus Burckhardt

The above instance of contrarian wisdom, from Ibn' Arabi's *Wisdom of the Prophets,* strikes the right note for a discussion of the Enneagram of Personality Types. This is so because the Enneagram does not lend itself to a superficial creed of self-fulfillment. Rather, it cuts deep, sure and true, refusing to flatter the vanities of the ego. The Enneagram unmasks, exposes and confronts. It threatens complacency. It teaches of the depths, the abyss, the sub-surface realities that play so big a role in shaping the outer person. It brings "distress," it empties conceits, it punctures pretentions. Then, after psychic space has been cleared and opened to new energies, it points the way to integrated and authentic living.

In performing this "work," the Enneagram hews to traditional wisdom. In the processes which it maps there is a pattern of "dying to the self," of the burial of a seed in the dark and damp earth, only to be followed by the emergence of that seed in the form of a thriving and spreading tree beneath the sun and the sky.

"The way to be immortal is to dye (sic) daily."[1] For this reason, Holy Scripture says "the man who loves his life will lose it" (John

---

[1] Sir Thomas Browne, *Religio Medici,* p. 71

12:25). This is why Christian baptism is about dying and being buried—as well as about rising—with Jesus Christ. This is why St. Augustine warns against the wiles of self. He says to "flee thyself, and
come to Him who made thee. For by fleeing thyself thou followest
thy true self, and by following thy true self thou cleavest to Him who
made thee."

The discipline of the Enneagram is a superb and subtle means of
entering the inner work that seeks after real change, real
transformation. It outlines a method by which to explore one's soul
in detail, with thoroughness and accuracy. It draws the soul and its
unhappy traits through a complex sieve, ferreting out the compulsions
and blindnesses that ensnare us. It lays bare the soul to the One "who
searches our hearts" (Romans 8:27). It makes room for that very One
to cleanse and purge, uplift and reconcile.

The Enneagram of Personality Types is of a two-fold nature,
involving first a symbol **(see diagram one)** consisting of a circle
enclosing both an equilateral triangle and an irregular hexagram, and,
second, a thorough body of knowledge that elucidates the dynamics
mapped upon the symbol. The geometric figures are arranged so as
to produce nine equidistant points on the circumference of the circle,
each point representing a personality type.

At its most profound, the Enneagram elaborates a technique that
assists in ordering one's relations with the Divine. In this, it presents
itself as a genuine form of *esotericism*, as a genuine specimen of that
knowledge and method that has long been used to explore human
interiority and to trace its affinities with the *exoteric*, or outer, realms.
In this technique, the inward and the outward, the spiritual and the
material, intertwine. There is a clear continuity with the hermetic
emblem, "As above, so below." (*Hermetic*, after the ancient texts that
comprise the *Hermetica*).

The word "esotericism" derives from the Greek "esoterikos,"
meaning "inner." As explained by Antoine Faivre,[2] the lexical content
of the word is scant, consisting of "eso," which means "inside," and
"ter," which implies an opposition. Scant though it may be, this content

---

[2] *Access to Western Esotericism,* p. 4

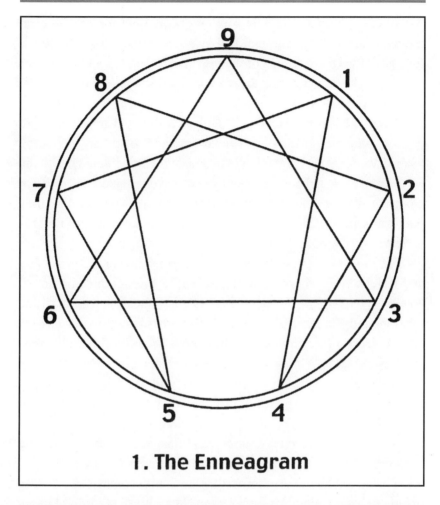

1. The Enneagram

hints at the essential meaning of the word, at its sense of human interiority, at its focus on the workings of the soul. In this, it corresponds to the inward gaze of the Enneagram.

In his introduction to the subject of esotericism, Faivre writes that the word refers ultimately to "a form of thought" consisting of six characteristics, four of them "intrinsic." These four are:

- Correspondences,
- Living nature,
- Imagination and mediations,
- Experience of transmutation.

The Enneagram is congruent with each. *

By correspondences, Faivre refers to the doctrine of universal interdependence, wherein real and symbolic connections are found to exist between the realms of the *microcosm* (man as a miniature or *epitome* of the universe) and the *macrocosm* (the universe itself). "The entire universe," he says, "is a huge theater of mirrors, an ensemble of hieroglyphs to be decoded."[3] Holy Scripture, it may be noted, evokes something of this doctrine at a number of points, including Psalm 19: 1-3, wherein the Divine is made manifest in nature, to the edification of man the microcosm: "The heavens declare the glory of God; the skies proclaim the work of his hands. Day after day they pour forth speech; night after night they display knowledge. There is no speech or language where their voice is not heard."

The Enneagram bases itself on correspondence between symbol and psyche. It is a symbolic mirror and a hieroglyph (a form of "pictorial writing") in which the psyche is limned, a symbol of the relations and dynamics of the inner life. It provides a map that unveils otherwise opaque phenomena. "The heart is deceitful above all things and beyond cure. Who can understand it?" (Jer 17:9). With the help of the Enneagram, one *can* understand it, "deceitfulness" notwithstanding. The Enneagram points to a "cure" as it ferrets out the wiles and strategies of the heart. Even more, the Enneagram resonates with the universe outside the human microcosm, suggesting affinities with nature in its entirety and even with supernature.

"Living nature" bears similarities to "correspondences." Living nature, rich in revelation, is to be "read" like a book. Nature is known to be "alive" in all its parts, with sympathies and antipathies linking its manifold particulars. The natural "talismans" discovered in this realm are useful in reestablishing the "physical or psychological harmony that [has] been disturbed."[4]

The Enneagram is itself a kind of "talisman" (an object or figure whose presence exercises a marked influence on human feelings or actions), a symbol and a body of knowledge useful in reestablishing the harmony and balance necessary to wholistic living. This restoration of balance is suggested by the "living" geometry of the symbol itself—

---

[3] *Access to Western Esotericism,* p. 10
[4] Ibid, p. 11

by the dynamic sense of the interconnections within and between the triangle and the hexagram—and realized as one ascends to a state of integration or descends to a state of disintegration.

The category of "imaginations and mediations" draws the individual into the realm of "rituals, symbolic images, mandalas, intermediary spirits."[5] It is a realm that is cognitive and visionary, making use of "the inner eye" to develop relationships with the intermediary world (the realm between spirit and matter, heaven and earth). This use of imagination and mediations serves as a tool to explore that most difficult of terrains, the human psyche.

As a symbol of surprising potency, the Enneagram is in fact a mandala-like structure (that is, a geometric representation of the microcosmos—or man—and his relations with the Divine, the cosmos and himself), with a complex and probing message. Like a mandala, it is a model of existence, a tool to facilitate self-development, a mirror to reflect the levels of self-consciousness, even "an instrument for transforming demonic forces."[6]

Finally, there is the "experience of transmutation." Herein is found a metamorphosis that allows "no separation between knowledge (gnosis) and inner experience, or intellectual activity and active imagination if we want to turn lead into silver or silver into gold... [In transmutation one is addressed by an] illuminated knowledge that favors the 'second birth.'"[7]

The Enneagram concurs with this experience, guiding the faculties of the psyche in a wholistic direction, requiring the active imagination (with its aptitude for the symbolic) and the discursive reason (calling to mind the verbal content of Enneagram theory) to work in tandem to unfold a change in personality. In this, the deep energies of the psyche are rechanneled and manifested as something altogether new. "Create in me a new heart...a new and right spirit within me" (Psalm 50:10). This can happen, bringing peace and balance. "For anyone who enters God's rest also rests from his own work, just as God did from his. Let us therefore make every effort to enter that rest" (Hebrews 4:10-11).

---

[5] *Access to Western Esotericism,* p. 12

[6] Klausbernd Vollmar, *The Secret of Enneagrams,* p. 31

[7] *Access to Western Esotericism,* p. 13

Labor, "work," is required, but work that lifts the leaden dissimilarity of living in the ego and replaces it increasingly with "rest," with the light, easy balance that can only be found in one's essence (in one's basic, deepest nature, in one's "spirit").

In this process, the individual finds intimations of his or her true destiny: unification with essence within the Divine Essence. The subject becomes what he "really is;" he penetrates to the core of his being within the context of transcendent reality. Prior to this unification, he remains "outside," living in the realm of "existence" (from *ex-sistere*, "remain out of").[8]

In all of this, the Enneagram harnesses the power of symbolic imagination. Symbols devolve from a higher sphere, a sphere impenetrable to profane reason and unable to be distilled into scientific concepts. In spite of—or because of—this, they are capable of reaching to the deepest levels of the self. The Enneagram, like other authentic symbols, helps the individual gain control over the turbulent sea of the egoic self and the unconscious forces that feed it.

The Enneagram, as symbol, effects its "magic" through internal communication, through wordless messages that evoke the inner structure of the psyche and its dynamics, as well as the transcendent realities amidst which the psyche draws life. According to G. I. Gurdjieff, who introduced the symbol to Europe from the Near East early in the 20th century, the Enneagram's equilateral triangle evokes the presence of "higher forces" while the six-sided figure signifies the human person. In this, the Enneagram plays a mediating role between nature (both micro- and macrocosmic) and supernature. "As above, so below."

In today's cultural climate, awash in profane symbols, a genuine symbol like the Enneagram stands out boldly. It bears the signature of reality and is found fruitful in its applications. It marries symbol and detailed body of knowledge; it enlists both imagination and reason. It mystifies and intrigues, resonates and attracts, drawing the subject into previously unexplored realms, giving birth to ("engendering") deep understandings of the inner life.

---

[8] Jean Borella, *Modern Esoteric Spirituality*, p. 346

In this, the Enneagram carries the sort of transformative power that Giordano Bruno attributed to symbols. Bruno, the Renaissance philosopher, drew and meditated upon numerous mandala-type structures. He possessed an abiding interest in one structure in particular.** "Bruno pointed out that if one meditated on this chemically real mandala for years, one unified one's own inner personality and saved one's soul from extraverted distractions and dissociation."[9]

The Enneagram has a like effect.

* The two secondary components of esotericism as a form of thought are, according to Faivre, "The Praxis of the Concordance" and "Transmission." The first refers to a tendency to establish common denominators between two or more sacred traditions or even among many traditions, in the hope of gaining "an illumination" of superior quality. The Enneagram of Personality Types is itself such a "common denominator." It is able to "read the soul" in ways that enrich the inner life of the devotees of a variety of sacred traditions.

The second refers to the transmission of an authentic esoteric teaching from master to disciple, using valid and preestablished means to initiate the disciple, frequently with an element of secrecy. In the case of the Enneagram of Personality Types, the earliest transmission (by the seminal theorist on the subject, Oscar Ichazo) was most likely effected according to such a paradigm. Owing to the wide and very public transmission of the subject as developed by subsequent authors and teachers representing a variety of perspectives—a transmission by means of books, workshops and trainings—the "initiations" that occur tend to be informal in nature.

** The author's investigations have failed to identify the structure in question. It is of interest, however, that Bruno (1548-1600) was a devotee of the work of the Franciscan Raymond Lull (1235?-1315), in whose voluminous works one can find Enneagrams. (Lull's Enneagrams, however, are far more complex than the symbol that is used today). It is noteworthy also that Lull catalogs nine virtues and nine vices,[10] which is suggestive of the Enneagram of Personality

[9] Marie-Louise Von Franz, *Alchemical Active Imagination*, p. 38

Types. The following comments by historian Dorothea Waley Singer hint at further connections: "Bruno expounds an elaborate myth... Progress, we are told, is not direct from one to another form. Rather— by an image reminiscent of the writings of Raymond Lull—change may be likened to motion around a wheel, so that each in turn is illuminated by the object in which converge the trinity of perfections... Thus is revealed to us the ultimate harmony of the whole, the true meaning of the nine spheres. We see that the beginning of one is the end of another."[11] One cannot, of course, assume that the "chemically real mandala" mentioned by Von Franz is in fact an Enneagram, yet the quoted portions from Singer's work are suggestive of a sensibility that is responsive to Ennea-type structures and dynamics.

---

[10]see Anthony Bonner, editor and translator, *Doctor Illuminatus: A Ramon Llull Reader,* pp. 333-334)
[11] *Giordano Bruno: His Life and Thought,* p. 131

2

Shadow and Reality

*"Our wisdom, if it is to be thought genuine, consists
almost entirely of two parts:
the knowledge of God and of ourselves."*
—John Calvin

Sir Thomas Browne, the pious litterateur and Paracelsian, explored "the cosmography of...self"[12] with uncommon honesty and diligence. He did so in the context of age-old certitudes, in which human beings (consisting of spirit, soul and body) were seen as three-fold reflections of the Divine Trinity. He embraced the venerable notion of microcosm and macrocosm, the suggestive symbolism of trinities, triads and ternaries, and other aspects of hermetic wisdom even then being lost to the profane methodology of early modern philosophy and science.

Relying on this wisdom, he was convinced the visible world is a picture of the invisible world, the earth a reflection of heaven. He believed, too, that the essence (or spirit) of each human being has its heavenly archetype, and that each spirit has in some mysterious fashion preceded the creation of the universe. "There is surely a piece of Divinity in us, something that was before the Elements, and owes no homage unto the Sun. Nature tells me I am the Image of God, as well as Scripture."[13] In this, he echoes closely the teaching of scripture:

---

[12]*Religio Medici*, p. 27
[13] Ibid, p. 116

"For he chose us in him before the creation of the world" (Ephesians 1:4).

This "piece of divinity" (or "essence" or "spirit" or "image of God") is but a part of the tripartite nature of the human being. The soul and the body are the other parts. Such "three-ness" is significant in traditional wisdom. In arithmology, for instance, it is a tenet that three forces are necessary to form a given phenomenon. Similarly, in Plato's *Timaeus* (31b), we learn "it is not possible to combine two things properly without a third to bond them."[14] In the Bible, it says "A cord of three strands is not quickly broken" (Ecclesiastes 4:12). And, according to Gerhard Dorn, the Christian alchemist, "The whole world has its form from the holy *ternarius* number three in its order and measure... the *one* unites, with its simplicity, the *two* into a *three*, and gives them a soul."[15] In the traditional view, the macrocosm is tripartite, as well, consisting of the informal (that which is beyond form), the subtle and the gross.

In the tripartite view of the human person **(see diagram two),** the spirit, soul and body are distinctive, substantive entities, even though they are also intertwined. Although minimized or denied in non-traditional thought, this view has scriptural grounding (italics added in following quotations):

- 1 Thessalonians 5:23, "May your whole *spirit, soul* and *body* be kept blameless."
- Luke 1: 46-47, "My *soul* glorifies the Lord and my *spirit* rejoices in God my saviour."
- Hebrews 4:12, "For the word of God is living and active. Sharper than any double-edged sword, it penetrates even to dividing *soul* and *spirit*, joints and marrow."
- Genesis 2:7, "The Lord God formed the man from the dust of the ground and breathed into his nostrils the *breath (spirit)* of life, and the man became a living being (or *living soul)*."

---

[14] Arthur Versluis, *Song of the Cosmos: An Introduction to Traditional Cosmology,* p. 133

[15] Marie-Louise von Franz, *Alchemical Active Imagination*, p. 42

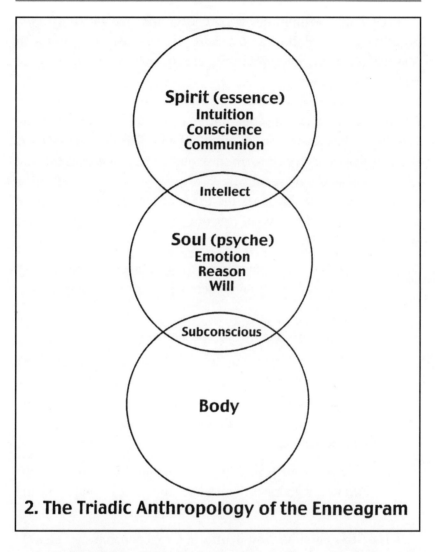

Spirit (essence)
Intuition
Conscience
Communion

Intellect

Soul (psyche)
Emotion
Reason
Will

Subconscious

Body

2. The Triadic Anthropology of the Enneagram

In 1 Corinthians 6:19, St. Paul refers to the human body as "a temple of the Holy Spirit, who is in you." This evokes the tripartite symbolism of the Solomonic temple, with its correspondences of sanctuary (spirit), inner temple (soul) and porch (body).

God is triune, and we are made in his image. We are made with a spirit like his. In the spirit, we fellowship with God. The Bible urges us to "walk" in the spirit, not in the soul. The spirit, in its turn, inspires the soul and the soul rules the body. Such is the ideal order, beginning "from above"—from whence the Holy Spirit descends like a dove into our spirits.

In St. Paul's writings, the transcendent principle within a person is "pneuma" (Greek for *spirit, breath*). He contrasts this spirit with "psyche" (*soul*), the latter word being used to refer to the psychological aspects of our nature.

Both spirit and soul contain triads within themselves. In the spirit, the faculties are intellect (or intuition), communion and conscience. In the soul, they are reason, emotion and will. The soul, in this view, is the mediating entity between spirit and body. It serves as the seat of man's conscious personality.

The Enneagram elaborates the triads of the soul into nine basic personality types: These types **(see diagram 3)** and their basic traits are, in brief:

- The Two—Generous, nurturing, friendly, helpful, flattering, possessive, vainglorious, coercive, histrionic, manipulative and hysterical.

- The Three—Appealing, accomplished, efficient, industrious, narcissistic, competitive, image-conscious, shallow, deceitful, malicious, vengeful.

- The Four—Authentic, original, individualistic, artistic, sensitive, romantic, introverted, self-absorbed, alienated, depressive, self-destructive.

- The Five—Visionary, perceptive, dispassionate, analytical, self-sufficient, withdrawn, cynical, iconoclastic, eccentric, phobic and paranoid.

- The Six—Faithful, dutiful, affectionate, cooperative, vigilant, cautious, belligerent, insecure, suspicious, fearful and defiant.

- The Seven—Enthusiastic, multi-talented, cheerful, optimistic, acquisitive, uninhibited, hyperactive, moody, excessive, debauched and self-destructive.

- The Eight—Strong, bold, commanding, magnanimous, independent, dominating, boastful, ruthless, reckless, vengeful and violent.

• The Nine—Accepting, serene, balanced, supportive, complacent, disengaged, resigned, stubborn, undeveloped, neglectful and ineffectual.

• The One—Principled, moral, conscientious, fair, orderly, impersonal, rigid, fussy, intolerant, self-righteous and punitive.

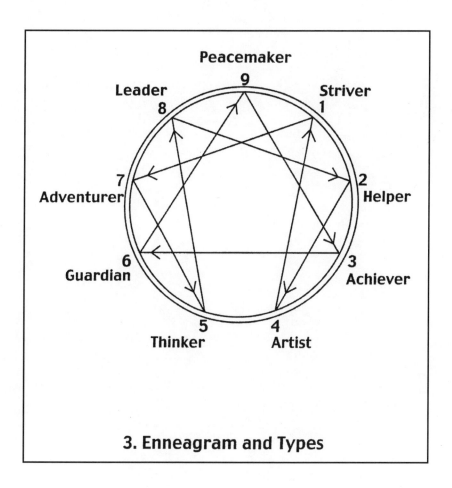

3. Enneagram and Types

3

The Helper

The Two, the Helper, is on the "wing" of the Triad of Emotion. Obedient to the conscience and its demand to help others, this type (when healthy) embodies empathy, compassion and warm-heartedness. There is a nurturing quality; twos drip with "the milk of human kindness."

Twos want to be used for good. They are ready to stand in the place of Jesus and say, "Come to me all you who are weary and burdened, and I will give you rest" (Matthew 11:28).

In scripture, broadly speaking, the number two affirms *difference;* it points to the *other* for good or ill. "The *two* may be, though different in character, yet one as to testimony and friendship... help and deliverance."[16]

This speaks well of the type.

"But, alas! where man is concerned, this number testifies of his fall, for it more often denotes that difference which implies *opposition, enmity,* and *oppression.*"[17]

This indicates a less attractive side of the type.

Veiled "enmity" or no, Type Two wishes to be the world's leading provider of "help and deliverance." There is in this wish an element of pride that can be the downfall of the type. There is, in this wish, an impulse for Twos to run themselves ragged in the attempt to do good

---

[16] E. W. Bullinger, *Number in Scripture,* p. 92
[17] Ibid

deeds. After all, as they see it, the world is waiting to be healed. It is a place of neediness, pain and affliction, pleading for their gifts. In response, they must be out and about, generous souls rushing to the rescue ("I feel your pain"). They are life's "bleeding heart liberals," dispensing healing, compassion and good will.

The Two is a "heart type," an outgoing feeling type who not only loves but who wants to be loved in turn. As a result, Helpers are prone to inflate their self-worth, with a desire for attention. In this, they play the martyr. Assuming their own virtue, they instill guilt and belittle others. ("Self-sacrifice enables us to sacrifice other people without blushing."—George Bernard Shaw). They can be showy, "gushy," overly intimate and possessive. Yet they deny their aggressive motives, their anger and bitterness when others do not respond the way they want them to.

Elements of the Two can be seen in Karen Horney's "self-effacing solution," in which she observes that the subject's "idealized image of himself primarily is a composite of 'lovable' qualities, such as unselfishness, goodness, generosity, humility, saintliness, nobility, sympathy. Helplessness, suffering, and martyrdom are also secondarily glorified... a premium is also placed on feelings—feelings of joy or suffering, feelings not only for individual people but for humanity... To have deep feelings is part of his image."[18]

The capital sin of Twos is pride. In their desire to be loved and admired for their good deeds and self-sacrifice, they put themselves not others at the center of interest. Religious belief can reinforce this tendency, as Twos come to see themselves as saints, set apart for special service—for all the world to see. God, it would seem, is hardly needed when a Two is on the scene.

In fact, it *is* the tendency of Helpers to see themselves as more than helpers. They see themselves as God-like, if not in theory at least in practice. As prideful people, they see themselves as the source and center of their own lives and of the lives of others. They want to give as only God can give.

---

[18]*Neurosis and Human Growth: The Struggle Toward Self-Realization,* pps. 222-223

Helpers can develop many selves in the attempt to meet the needs of others. This can be a good thing (as in the Apostle Paul's becoming "all things to all men" in an effort to rescue them) when centered in a healthy sense of self. When this tendency emerges from a fragmented self out of touch with its own depths, it can sow mischief.

If truth be told, Twos are as needy as anyone else. Unlike the other types, though, they suppress their own needs and project them onto others ("projection"—the tendency to ascribe to another person the feelings, thoughts, or attitudes present in oneself, or to regard outer reality as embodying the same). They are convinced that others need their help—whether those others want it or not. Sometimes the help is accepted, even though it may be inappropriate. In such instances it feeds into the weaknesses of the recipient, promoting a co-dependent relationship.

Average and unhealthy Twos approach others in an overly emotional manner. They put personal considerations above abstract ideas, human need above "the rules." They can be bubbly and hovering, swooping down on their chosen prey. They can be intrusive, invading the space of others. They may want to chat at awkward times or may exaggerate their emotions to excite the interest of others.

Affected and theatrical, Twos are skilled in flattery. They are keenly aware of how others feel about them and equally sensitive to the things that flatter others. Attentive and eager to please, they become effusive and doting. They allow their feelings to have the upper hand even as reason is minimized. "Nothing disturbs feeling so much as thinking. It is therefore understandable that in this [extroverted feeling] type thinking will be kept in abeyance as much as possible."[19] Indeed, thinking becomes an "appendage" to feeling.[20] As a result, Twos develop neither a realistic view of others nor a sober judgment of themselves.

The speech of Twos is frequently vague. ("He's *such* a wonderful person.") It is speech designed to please others rather than to communicate substance. It tends to be "lip labor" (Jacob Boehme)

---

[19]C. G. Jung, *Psychological Types,* p. 357
[20] Ibid

and little else. Thus Twos, speaking empty words, expend a lot of energy in flattering others even as they seek for themselves the attention, praise and reassurance of those others. They are, in fact, often wrapped up in themselves and barely hear what others are trying to say. "He who answers before listening—that is his folly and his shame" (Proverbs 18:13).

Twos, often sweet, cute and "precious," can be seductive, exhibiting an allure that draws others. They may share intimacies, dropping comments about their private lives as a means of drawing others closer to them. There is a desire for sexual attention as a sign of approval, an erotic invitation that seeks to affirm one's self worth. In this the Two, as elsewhere, can become invasive and smothering, putting off others rather than attracting them.

Helpers, in such a mode, can become possessive and over-involved. They do this as a way of manipulating a person and drawing that person away from others. The person singled out is jealously guarded. The Two wishes to be the prime influence on the person in question; others are to remain at arm's-length.

In being possessive, Helpers can be dominating, demanding and coercive; they can be impatient, quick with advice, eager to direct the lives of others—all in the name of love. In this, again, they "need to be needed;" they need to be loved for all they do. As self-appointed martyrs, they feel entitled to the gratitude of others and they will put "in their place" anyone who disagrees with their attempts to help. ("If you had listened to *my* advice, everything would have worked out okay.")

Helpers can be condescending towards others in an obvious manner. This tendency indicates an assumed superiority on the part of the Two, which fits the notion of the self-proclaimed saint. Again, the motive is probably a moral one-upmanship, not the welfare of the other.

When discouraged, Twos may seek the love they think is due them by becoming hypochondriacs, suffering a breakdown or developing emotionally based illnesses. This is not a wholly unexpected development in an emotional type like the Two. Angry because their own needs (as they define them) have not been met, hurt because others have not responded "as they should" to the Two's benevolence, and lacking the ability to obtain the help they need, Twos may turn their aggressions inward and make themselves ill. Of course, others will get the blame.

The epistolary Archbishop of Cambrais addresses—with keen insight—a correspondent with a type Two personality:

> You have spent all your life in the belief that you are wholly devoted to others, and never self-seeking. Nothing so feeds self-conceit as this sort of internal testimony that one is quite free from self-love, and always generously devoted to one's neighbors. But all this devotion that seems to be for others is really for yourself. Your self-love reaches to the point of perpetual self-congratulation that you are free from it; all your sensitiveness is lest you might not be fully satisfied with self; this is at the root of all your scruples. It is the 'I' which makes you so keen and sensitive. You want God as well as man to be always satisfied with you, and you want to be satisfied with yourself in all your dealings with God.
>
> Besides, you are not accustomed to be contented with a simple good will—your self-love wants a lively emotion, a reassuring pleasure, some kind of charm or excitement. You are too much used to be guided by imagination and to suppose that your mind and will are inactive, unless you are conscious of their workings. And thus you are dependent upon a kind of excitement similar to that which the passions arouse, or theatrical representations... It is mere self-love to be inconsolable at seeing one's own imperfections; but to stand face to face with them, neither flattering nor tolerating them, seeking to correct oneself without becoming pettish—this is to desire what is good for its own sake and for God's.
>
> Thus the great Fénelon.[21]

The disintegrating Helper, adrift in unhappy straits, is only half of the picture. The other half represents a person who is truly unselfish

---

[21]quoted by Aldous Huxley, *The Perennial Philosophy,* pps. 253-254

towards others. The better angels of the healthy Two are found in a person who is amiable, delightful, loveable, charming, solicitous... all the things a good and helpful person should be. Such an exemplar, devoted to the genuine welfare of those around him or her ("Love must be sincere."—Romans 12:9), is generous to a fault. Ever on the lookout for persons in need, these Twos are sensitive and responsive. They know that it is more blessed to give than to receive. Their concern is not so much that they will be loved as that they can provide for those who really need a helping hand.

In their concern for others, healthy Helpers are nurturing, providing the encouragement, nourishment and all-around support that individuals need at various stages of life. Healthy Twos offer advice in a non-judgmental and understanding way. They learn to recognize what others really need and want and then help them to achieve their proper ends. Warmhearted and outgoing, they express in a vital way their love and concern for others. In this, they do right by God and by their brothers and sisters, "for he who loves his fellow man has fulfilled the law" (Romans 13:8). Helpers at this stage have learned the meaning of caring and, even more, of humility, and are living out these virtues for the good of all.

In scripture, Mary the mother of Jesus appears to be a Two. Of course, the Bible nowhere gives anything like a full account of an individual's personality; rather, one catches but glimpses of various figures and the actions in which they engage. There are exceptions, however, among them the portraits of Jesus and David. The details of the personality of Jesus can be seen from many angles in the Gospels. In the case of David, not only does a detailed portrait emerge from the narrative of his dramatic life, but he can be seen "from the inside" in the Psalms that are credited to him.

Scripture does, in its presentation of the archaic figures who peopled the Mediterranean World and the Near East two, three and four-thousand years ago, carry within itself a sort of "archetypal" (original pattern or first form) aspect in relation to psychological type. The patterns of human personality can be discerned in the sacred writings, if not in detail at least in broad strokes. These personalities are, as it were, "prototypes" of what one sees in the world today, larger-than-life figures in many cases but true to life all the same.

Mary the mother of Jesus appears to have been a dedicated Helper, a healthy Two. Her devoted service was rendered to her God and to her Son. A humble maiden, she submitted to God and she praised God for the honor He had accorded her. She kept the mysteries made known to her "hidden in her heart." Her service in the great scheme of salvation history, acquitted with grace and humility, extended even to a faithful recollection of certain of the facts of the salvation story, as she is the most likely source of the infancy narratives revealed years after the event.

Despite her virtues and holy service, Mary's humanness is evident in a number of passages. Though surrounded by signs of the supernatural, she seemed at times to be unaware of her son's mission and his single-minded dedication to that mission. When she and Joseph found their 12-year-old son in the temple courts after he had been missing several days—found him discoursing as an equal among the teachers of religion—they did not grasp the meaning of his statement that he "had to be in [his] Father's house." Nor, at the wedding in Cana, did Mary understand that her son's "hour" had not come when she, somewhat imperiously, enlisted him to rescue a party running short of wine. Again, she and the brothers of Jesus on more than one occasion came to take him away after others had claimed he was "beside himself" and possessed by Beelzebub.

Jesus was himself a Helper, readily available throughout his ministry to teach and heal and feed the crowds who came to him. At the same time, this "man for others" was not opposed to taking time for himself, time to recollect what had occurred in his mission and to plan for what lay ahead, time to be alone with the Father. "Very early in the morning, while it was still dark, Jesus got up, left the house and went off to a solitary place, where he prayed." (Mark 1:35). Jesus needed to be alone with the Father, to rest and reflect and be refreshed. The Two needs to do the same. There are times—more times than the Two is willing to admit—when God's will for His servants is to put their own needs first, to put rest and food and even play ahead of waiting on others. The Two might see this as little short of heresy but it is true nonetheless.

Another problem area: the warnings in scripture about drawing attention to oneself. The Helper tends to do just this, as he or she relishes being noticed for doing good deeds. This is not the Christian way, according to the Sermon on the Mount. "So when you give to the needy, do not announce it with trumpets, as the hypocrites do in the synagogues and on the streets, to be honored by men. I tell you the truth, they have received their reward in full. But when you give to the needy, do not let your left hand know what your right hand is doing, so that your giving may be in secret. Then your Father, who sees what is done in secret, will reward you." (Matthew 6:1-4).

Jesus also warns about wrong motives in the prayer life and in the practice of fasting. In both cases, the temptation to parade one's virtue before others is firmly rebuked and the believer is urged to practice his devotions with regard to God only. Again, "Your Father, who sees what is done in secret, will reward you." (vss 6 and 18).

As noted above, Twos can be careless in their speech. A sort of "rote" flattery, superficial and insincere, serves as a means of manipulating others. It is perilous to the soul of the Two and potentially harmful to others. "Whoever flatters his neighbor is spreading a net for his feet" (Proverbs 29:5). The "neighbor" may take the flattery seriously, puffing him with pride and leading to unhappy results.

Jesus, too, takes the words a person speaks with utmost seriousness: "But I tell you that men will have to give account on the day of judgment for every careless word they have spoken. For by your words you will be acquitted, and by your words you will be condemned." (Matthew 12:36). An arresting thought, this, linking careless words and the day of judgment. Simple honesty is the best course. "Let your 'Yes' be 'Yes,' and your 'No,' 'No.'" (Matthew 5:37).

Helpers, in swelling pride, view themselves as saviours of the world, called to shower good deeds on the helpless and the needy and those who stand in want of advice on all manner of things. As Christians, though, they would be wise to temper their desire to be of help with an awareness that God is already at work, helping and sustaining and providing, even in the worst of circumstances. "Because of the LORD'S great love we are not consumed, for his compassions never fail. They are new every morning; great is your faithfulness" (Lamentations 3:22-23). Even in Israel's darkest hour, the Lord was close by, compassionate and caring. And as the Apostle Paul reminds his readers, "He who did not spare his own Son, but gave him up for us all—how will he not also, along with him, graciously give us all things" (Romans 8:32). The Two's efforts are often necessary but need to be made, and understood, in the context of God's outworking in personal lives and the history of the world. The Two needs to let God love through him or her, not attempt to stand in the place of God. Twos need to realize they are required to trust and serve God first, knowing all the while that God is working out His purposes.

Paul sets an example in Colossians, wherein he stresses the need for wisdom, not simply good intentions; for awareness of the Divine Presence and His centrality in all the activities of life, and for gratitude: "Let the word of Christ dwell in you richly as you teach and admonish one another with all wisdom, and as you sing psalms, hymns and spiritual songs with gratitude in your hearts to God. And whatever you do, whether in word or deed, do it all in the name of the Lord Jesus, giving thanks to God the Father through him." (3:16-17). The Two, tending to stress emotion over logic, feeling over principle, needs the corrective of just such a firm and settled—and joyful—wisdom.

Jesus himself set the pattern for the healthy Helper, again and again, in his life and doctrine. In one example, he draws a contrast between the power-idolatry of the Roman world, with all of its pomp and hero-worship, and the importance of service, an emphasis to which the the Two should resonate: "You know that those who are regarded as rulers of the Gentiles lord it over them, and their high officials exercise authority over them. Not so with you. Instead, whoever wants to become great among you must be your servant, and whoever wants to be first must be slave of all. For even the Son of Man did not come to be served, but to serve, and to give his life as a ransom for many." (Mark 10: 42-45).

In the 12th chapter of Romans, Paul offers solid guidance to those—such as Twos—who are eager to be engaged in well-doing. He touches on the humility, clear thinking and faith necessary to the authentic service of others. He touches, too, on the awareness of one's gifts and the need to exercise them in community: "For by the grace given to me, I say to every one of you: Do not think of yourself more highly than you ought, but rather think of yourself with sober judgment, in accordance with the measure of faith God has given you... We have different gifts, according to the grace given us. If a man's gift is prophecying, let him use it in proportion to his faith. If it is serving, let him serve; if it is teaching, let him teach; if it is encouraging, let him encourage; if it is contributing to the needs of others, let him give generously; if it is leadership, let him govern diligently; if it is showing mercy, let him do it cheerfully." (Vss 3, 6-8).

The grace of God accounts for varied gifts, distributed as He wills among the personality types. The Helper's gifts, recognizable in the preceding passage, are most evident in serving, encouraging, showing mercy, giving generously. The Helper, prone to pride, would like to be all things to all men. This will not happen. The Helper, however, does embody gifts essential to building up the Body of Christ. And there is a gift in store "to those who by persistence in doing good seek glory, honor and immortality" (Romans 2:7). For to them "he will give eternal life" (Ibid.)

4

The Achiever

"One's real life is often the life that one does not lead."
—Oscar Wilde

Achievers, in the middle of the "heart center" (the Triad of Emotion), are seekers of success. In their quest for worldly attainment, they are among life's "stars," displaying a charismatic quality that can both inspire and manipulate others, produce good or work evil.

Their capacity for good or bad is reflected in the number Three itself, which on the one hand "stands for the mortal condition, the disturbed, intermediate condition to which time and space belong,"[22] and, on the other hand, "for that which is *solid, real, substantial, complete,* and *entire.*"[23] Thus the enneatype appears in paradoxical guises: unhealthy in one state and healthy in another.

Achievers, in their single-minded quest for "success," can indeed display both "disturbed" and healthy traits. Both come into play as they dream of themselves at the top of their chosen field, often visualizing their route to success. Indeed, they are the prototype of the classmate voted "most likely to succeed." In their unhealthy states, winning is the only thing.

---

[22] Edmund D. Cohen, *C. G. Jung and the Scientific Attitude,* p. 89
[23] Bullinger, *Number in Scripture,* p. 107

As they seek status and acceptance, Achievers gauge keenly the responses of others, aiming to measure up to the criteria of success defined by their culture or subculture. They are, to this end, driven, controlled and aggressive. They are vigilant and self-reliant. Their lives revolve around "me, myself and I." They are prone to "hype" their abilities and accomplishments, while downplaying anything that would threaten their self-centered stance. They play a role, wear a mask. As a result, their inner self shrinks from awareness until only the outer shell remains.

The Achiever has no use for the cautionary wisdom of Ecclesiastes: "I have seen all the things that are done under the sun; all of them are meaningless, a chasing after the wind." (1:4). Such a vision is the Three's worst nightmare. To think that all of the fame and glory after which he or she chases could be "meaningless," to think it all a "Vanity Fair" and little more, that is asking more than the Three can bear. Threes are, after all, the last to comprehend the fleeting nature of fame; they are the last to realize their achievements will be rapidly forgotten; the last to fathom how little it all matters to other people in the first place.

In pursuing their dreams, Threes tend to activate their root sin, deceit. With great skill, they tell blatant lies or merely shade the truth, often without realizing it, so habitual does it become. Overall, they present a sublety of character, a smoothness. They fool not only others but themselves, thereby leaving their view of the inner and outer worlds distorted.

Achievers, smooth and self-obsessed, strive after success as defined by their social setting. They evaluate themselves in terms of it, measuring their personal worth by conformity to the approved criteria. They are career animals and social climbers, seeking superiority over others. They devote themselves to the surface of life ("All the vain things that charm me most"—Isaac Watts), refusing to look deeply into the meaning of existence. Of unhealthy Threes it can be said: "They exchanged the truth of God for a lie, and worshiped and served created things rather than the Creator." (Romans 1:5).

To reach their goals, Achievers must attract attention. They will not, if they can help it, work patiently behind the scenes, like a dutiful

Six. Rather, they are front and center, employing their skills at self-promotion. They shine as show business personalities, politicians, sales representatives or in any other occupation in which personality, presentation and an air of confidence are paramount. "Theirs is a star quality born of self-regard, self-respect, self certainty."[24]

Not surprisingly, Achievers are sophisticated and socially adept. They absorb the manners and nuances that are pleasing to those whom they hope to impress. They flow with ease in the social current. The right gesture, the apt phrase, come naturally. They develop many relationships but not many deep ones. They are well-groomed and often "sexy."

Achievers are skilled talkers. Unlike the Seven, however, the Three uses words to make a good impression and to reach long range goals. The Seven, by contrast, is more interested in charming or seducing others for short-term purposes. In neither case is much attention paid to the deeper meanings of language or the ideas they express.

Achievers are not all style over substance. They are, in many instances, the "genuine article," made to look even better than they are by their skillful self-promotion. They tend to be highly competent persons, qualified to meet the challenges in their area of expertise. They come prepared: advanced degrees, attendance at seminars, late hours at the office, whatever it takes to succeed. They work hard to shine before others.

Achievers identify completely with the enterprises to which they devote their time and energy. As surely as they have a one-track mind for success, they are clear as to the course to be followed. They do not waste time or resources but take aim at the chosen goal and pursue a straight-forward course. In doing so they are clear-minded in their judgments, setting helpful standards for themselves and others.

Achievers possess an inner dynamic that keeps them moving forward (when they are healthy and therefore balanced). They are infectious in their enthusiasm and readily attract others to their cause. As good team players they are adept at motivating others to aspire

---

[24] John M. Oldham, M. D., and Lois B. Morris, addressing the "self-confident style" in their *Personality Self-Portrait, Why You Think, Work, Love, and Act the Way You Do,* p. 79

after the same ends as they. They know the best way to reach the goal is by building a team that acts in a harmonious manner. With their competent air, verbal talent and organizational acumen, Threes can do just that. They bring success to those who labor with them, not to themselves only.

The words of Immanuel Kant point to the type: "Controlling the inclinations of other people in order to direct and manage them according to one's own intentions, almost amounts to being in possession of them as mere instruments of one's own will. It is not surprising, then, that striving after the faculty to have influence over others is a passion."[25]

The patriach Jacob, son of Isaac and grandson of Abraham, appears to be a Three. From his birth, he was in competition with his elder brother, Esau. Jacob, whose name means "heel-catcher" or "supplanter," held tight to his brother's heel even as Esau emerged from the womb, and he remained in pursuit of his brother's primacy in the years that followed. In this archetypal case of "sibling rivalry," Jacob was encouraged by his mother, Rebecca, who may have acted as she did owing to a revelation from God (Genesis 25:23). For her part, Rebecca played the role that mothers or mother-substitutes play in the lives of many Threes, serving as the nurturing figure who provides essential mirroring for the child. Jacob was a "momma's boy," frequenting the tents and pursuing the settled routines of life while his rougher, heartier brother became a man of the outdoors and a skilled huntsman. All the while, Jacob internalized his mother's favoritism.

Jacob first tricked his shortsighted brother into selling him his birthright. Later, with the connivance of his mother, he tricked his feckless father and received the blessing that should have gone to Esau. The elder brother, outraged, determined to kill Jacob. Jacob, warned by his mother, fled to Harran to live with his uncle, Laban.

On the way, Jacob experienced his famous dream, in which he saw angels ascending and descending a stairway—or "ladder"—to heaven. In the dream, the Lord promised Jacob a vast territory and

---

[25]*Anthropology from a Pragmatic Point of View,* p. 179

countless descendents (success indeed!). Jacob, deceiver though he was, received the divine favor.

In the years that followed, the exile came close to meeting his match in cunning and deceit in the person of his uncle. The wily Laban tricked his nephew into marrying his plain daughter, Leah, and contrived to get 14 years of work out of Jacob as the price of his marriage to both Leah and the beautiful Rachel. Yet, in the course of these dealings, Jacob's intelligence, industry and desire to succeed worked their magic and the younger man surpassed the older man in accumulating wealth.

At the prompting of the Lord, Jacob at last returned to Canaan, accompanied by his family and flocks, slaves and servants. (In parting with her father, Rachel became a deceiver like her husband, stealing Laban's household gods and then hiding them). As he neared his homeland, Jacob determined to mollify Esau by presenting him with generous gifts of livestock. Despite the gifts, Jacob's fear intensified when he was informed that his brother was approaching with four-hundred men. In the event, Esau was anything but vengeful. Weeping, Esau kissed his errant brother, forgave him his misdeeds and welcomed him. A deferential Jacob parleyed with Esau and then took leave of his brother, indicating he would follow him home. Deceiving his brother yet again, Jacob led his entourage in another direction.

The turning point in Jacob's life occurred on the eve of his reunion with Esau, when he "wrestled with God" on the banks of the River Jabbok. Jacob successfully sought a blessing but suffered a dislocated hip in the course of the struggle. Permanently lamed, this man of pride, self-reliance and cunning had at last met his match and yet, in yielding, received not only a blessing but a new name as well: Israel— "He who strives with God—and prevails." Wounded, broken, flawed... but blessed, Jacob was equipped to fulfill his role in salvation history.

Warnings against deceit, the root sin of the Three, are commonplace in scripture. In the Ten Commandments, there is the admonition against "bearing false witness" and, in Leviticus 19:11, one reads, "Do not steal. Do not lie. Do not deceive one another." The Psalmist, too, speaks God's impatience with falsehood: "How long will you love delusions and seek false gods" (4:2). Proverbs puts it pithily: "Better to be poor than a liar" (19:22).

Achievers need to heed the Word on this subject, as they are skilled at shading the truth and even outright lying as they strive to fulfill their ambitions by seeking the false gods of success, status and fame. They find their ambitions more desirable than straight talk. After all, if corners need to be cut, well, that's the way of the world. Yet... "Truth is one, and he who does the truth in the small thing is of the truth; he who will do it only in a great thing, who postpones the small thing near him to the great farther from him, is not of the truth."[26] The Three, in reaching for the top, ignores or downplays the little unsung acts of honesty that would add a human touch to an otherwise driven life. There is a crying need to learn the priority of honorable behavior, that "humility comes before honor" (Proverbs 18:12).

Jesus promised his followers they would know the truth and the truth would set them free. Achievers need to face the truth and to speak the truth, to let "their yea be yea and their nay be nay." "Anything beyond this comes from the evil one" (Matthew 5:37). They need to reorder their priorities, to become something more than "men of this world whose reward is in this life" (Psalm 17:14). They need to begin measuring their lives against the Word of God rather than the opinions of mankind.

As Achievers answer the call to conversion, they need not abandon their ambitions but need to pursue them in a larger framework and with a changed motivation. The framework is the spiritual life and the motivation is to use one's talents to glorify God, not self. They need to decide whom they will serve. Jesus Christ addresses the point in a teaching as well known as it is neglected: "No one can serve two masters. Either he will hate the one and love the other, or he will be devoted to the one and despise the other. You cannot serve both God and money" (Matthew 6:24).

Everyone who would walk the Christian walk must part with the world (the "world" in the sense of sinful man, dedicated to unrighteousness and hostile to God and truth). To be wedded to the fallen world is to be lost. Rather, "God wants us to walk in *obedience—*

---

[26] C. S. Lewis, *George MacDonald, An Anthology,* p. 36

not victory. Obedience is oriented toward God; victory is oriented toward self... This is not to say God doesn't want us to experience victory, but rather to emphasize that victory is a by-product of obedience."[27]

The unhealthy Three puts "victory" ahead of obedience, thus reversing proper priorities. The "recovering" Three, by contrast, gets the order right. The recovering Three opens—or *is* opened by—a supernatural grace; is opened to influences that are "otherworldly" rather than "worldly." "At the very moment of their call, [they] find that they have already broken with all the natural ties of life. This is not their own doing, but his who calls them. For Christ has delivered them from immediacy with the world, and brought them into immediacy with himself. We cannot follow Christ unless we are prepared to accept and affirm that breach as a *fait accompli.* It is no arbitrary choice on the disciple's part, but Christ himself, who compels him thus, to break with his past... We must face up to the truth that the call of Christ *does* set up a barrier between man and his natural life."[28]

Similarly, the Apostle Paul addressed the Corinthians, whose worldliness was the unhappy leaven of an otherwise Spirit-filled church. In 1 Corinthians, he urges believers to discern the spirits; he reminds them of their true benefactor. He says: "We have not received the spirit of the world but the Spirit who is from God, that we may understand what God has freely given us" (2:12). Gratitude reflects the spirit from above, envy and competition the spirit from below. Gratitude is owed to the good creation and its Creator; nothing is owed to the "world" and its prince.

Paul urges believers to curb their self-seeking and to look after the welfare of others, an unnatural inclination for unhealthy Achievers (and the human race at large): "Do nothing out of selfish ambition or vain conceit, but in humility consider others better than yourselves. Each of you should look not only to your own interests, but also to the interests of others" (Philippians 2:3-4). The believer needs to be aware that God does not choose only the VIPs of the world as his servants; often, it is the contrary: "Not many of you were wise by

---

[27] Jerry Bridges, *The Pursuit of Holiness,* p. 21
[28] Dietrich Bonhoeffer, *The Cost of Discipleship,* pps. 105-106

human standards; not many were influential; not many were of noble birth. But God chose the foolish things of the world to shame the wise; God chose the weak things of the world to shame the strong" (1 Corinthians 1:26-27). Who comes first, God or mammon? God or personal achievement? God or the applause of the crowd? Jesus answers this question in the Sermon on the Mount: "Therefore I tell you, do not worry about your life, what you will eat or drink; or about your body, what you will wear. Is not life more important than food, and the body more important than clothes?... So do not worry, saying, 'What shall we eat?' or 'What shall we drink?' or 'What shall we wear?' For the pagans run after all these things, and your heavenly Father knows that you need them. But seek first his kingdom and his righteousness, and all these things will be given to you as well" (Matthew 6:25, 31-33).

The priority is God's kindom and righteousness. To dwell in that kingdom, Threes need to put their personal ambitions in second place. This is, for the Three, to turn the world upside down. "For the message of the cross is foolishness to those who are perishing, but to us who are being saved it is the power of God" (1 Corinthians 1:18). The Three "who is being saved," by ordering his or her life in a Godward direction, often finds that the good things of creation follow in their turn. One receives the kindom "and all these things" are added to it.

There is no reason why a Christian of Type Three should not have healthy ambitions, or enjoy a well-earned reputation, or take pleasure in the good things of the earth. The Bible does not encourage its followers to wean themselves from the creation by suppressing their desires. Neither the Three nor any other type need fear such an unnatural teaching. "This barrier [between the Christian and the "world"] is no surly contempt for life, no legalistic piety, it is the life which is life indeed, the gospel, the person of Jesus Christ... He wants to be the centre, through him alone all things shall come to pass."[29] Creation is good: God made it. Rightly understood, the things of the creation (even the fallen creation we know, even the realm of nature that is "a good thing spoiled" in the words of C. S. Lewis) can and should be enjoyed.

---

[29] Bonhoeffer, p. 106

Achievers need to rediscover the inner reality they have suppressed. During a life devoted to worldly ambition, the public "persona" may have swollen with success while the person behind the mask, the deepest and truest self—the spirit made in the image of God's Spirit—has shriveled. The Three has been heedless that "this world in its present form is passing away" (1 Corinthians 7:31). Instead, he or she has chosen the transitory image without and neglected the enduring principle within.

By contrast, the teachings of Jesus point to the importance of the inner self. "For out of the overflow of the heart the mouth speaks. The good man brings good things out of the good stored up in him, and the evil man brings evil things out of the evil stored up in him" (Matthew 12:34-35).

Old Testament prophecy knew of the inner self, too: "'This is the covenant I will make with the house of Israel after that time,' declares the LORD. 'I will put my law in their minds and write it on their hearts'" (Jeremiah 31:33). A future interiority was foreseen for the people of God.

Paul, in his letter to the Romans, offers advice the Three can use: "Do not think of yourself more highly than you ought, but rather think of yourself with sober judgment, in accordance with the measure of faith God has given you" (12:3). "Sober judgment" is the key (as it is for the Two—and all other types as well); a balanced assessment that neither inflates the self nor unfairly punishes or diminishes it.

Achievers need to learn that good intentions, proper motivation, well-laid plans and great effort do not always lead to success. They have to make room for the possibility of failure and hardship without succumbing to despair. God allows testing. Jesus warned his followers that persecutions would come, and it is undeniable that persons who stand up for God in the most forthright manner can expect to incur the wrath of the crowd. "Blessed are you when people insult you, persecute you and falsely say all kinds of evil against you because of me. Rejoice and be glad, because great is your reward in heaven" (Matthew 5:11-12). Yes, the Three may be called to suffer affliction for Christ's sake, to take a "time out" from the relentless pursuit of the world's applause and stand up for spiritual truth. If so, it is a blessing, for it "is this that transmutes poverty of spirit into heavenly humility."[30]

The realization that the worldly armor worn by the seeker of status can be discarded, that the tactics of the social climber can be abandoned, allows a shifting of the emotional center towards the inner self that has for so long been neglected. The Three learns at last to "worship in spirit and in truth" (John 4:24), to forsake the idols of the market place and to put his faith where it belongs.

In thus changing his outlook the three may experience "An immense elation and freedom, as the outlines of the confining selfhood melt down."[31] The reason is that Threes, like other aggressive types, are in their average to unhealthy states almost totally unaware of their inner selves. Thus, in "conversion," when the depths are stirred, the transformation is more than likely to be sudden and emotionally charged. "These persons [the specific reference is to the somatotonic of William Sheldon's famous typology] are so intensely extraverted as to be quite unaware of what is happening in the lower levels of their minds. If for any reason their attention comes to be turned inwards, the resulting self-knowledge, because of its novelty and strangeness, presents itself with the force and quality of a revelation and their metanoia, or change of mind, is sudden and thrilling."[32]

Thus, when the depths are stirred like the pool of Bethesda, the transformation that follows is dramatic, a "revelation," a welling up of the spirit within. Wayward Threes are "born again"... and made ready to pursue the life of the kingdom, even as they have hitherto pursued the ephemeral life of the "world" and its conceits. They experience at last an abiding joy that displaces the counterfeits and brings in its stead the message of fulfillment.

---

[30] Benjamin B. Warfield, *Faith and Life,* p. 35
[31] William James, *The Varieties of Religious Experience,* p. 273
[32] Aldous Huxley, *The Perennial Philosophy,* pps. 155-156

5

The Artist

"Man is a make-believe animal—he is never so truly himself as when he is acting a part."
—William Hazlitt

The "Artist," the creative individual who occupies the space of the Four, bears in his person the symbolism of the number under which he is listed. "The number *four* ... follows the revelation of God in the Trinity, namely *His creative works*. He is known by the things that are seen."[33] Fours, made in the image of God, display their creative touch in a variety of ways, be it in a work of art, a special style of clothes, a fashionable apartment or impeccable manners. They are "known by the things that are seen."

Such "artists," however, bear a dark side as well. They are in their unhealthy states entangled by the poison vine of envy. They are envious above all of the apparent normalcy of others, of the easy involvement with day-to-day living that other people seem to enjoy.

Envy is first cousin to coveting, and either state leaves a person discontented. Whereas coveting eyes the possessions or attainments of others in the hope of having them for itself, envy does not wish so much to take for itself as it wishes to take away from others. The desire of the "evil eye" is to see mishap and misfortune visited upon the lives of those who are envied, to see the rich man lose his wealth, the desired woman her beauty, the "normal," contented family its happiness.

---

[33]Bullinger, *Number in Scripture,* p. 123

Artists, because they are sensitive, are troubled by such emotions. They try hard to understand why they are the way they are—why they envy, why they are depressed, why they are "different"—but tend to be emotional rather than logical in the effort, thereby finding few answers. According to Ole Hallesby, the melancholic personality (to which the Four is closely related) "is surely more self-centered than any of the other temperaments. He is inclined to that kind of self contemplation which paralyzes his will and energy. He is always dissecting himself and his own mental conditions, taking off layer after layer as an onion is peeled, until there is nothing direct and artless left in his life; there is only his everlasting self-examination. This self-examination is not only unfortunate, it is harmful. Melancholics usually drift into morbid mental conditions. They are concerned not only about their spiritual state; they are also unduly concerned about their physical condition. Everything that touches a melancholic is of prime importance to him, hence no other type can so easily become a hypochondriac."[34]

Fours, who inhabit a wing of the emotional or "heart" triad, absorb the attitudes of others, often in a distorted manner. By internalizing these unacceptable and threatening "vibes," they are left feeling anxious and out of balance, tempted to withdraw from others to shield their fragile emotional state. Yet even as they withdraw, they are well able to grasp immediately the facts of a social situation. They have an intuitive insight into things hidden from other personality types. Their immediacy of self-awareness (albeit subjective) is a pronounced trait, as is their insight into others.

This aptitude for insight, this ability to bypass the rigors of the reasoning process, is a valuable gift. "The peculiar nature of introverted intuition... produces a peculiar type of man: the mystical dreamer and seer on the one hand, the artist and the crank on the other. The artist might be regarded as the normal representative of this type."[35] Fours, as such, have an "Intuitive perception of the hidden analogies of things."[36]

---

[34] *Temperament and the Christian Life,* pps. 43-44
[35] C. G. Jung, *Psychological Types,* p. 401
[36] Hazlitt

According to Claudio Naranjo, M. D., Fours (more than the other types) are subject to "sexual envy," an inclination to partake of aspects of the opposite gender. To Naranjo, this envy (experienced by both men and women) is "striking in the case of the counter-sexual identification underlying homosexuality and lesbianism." He says these predilections are "more frequent in ennea-type IV than in any other character."[37]

Fours, as heart types dwelling next to the head center, are often lovers of beauty, in art or nature. On the outside they are refined and mannered, "special," in contrast to the turbulent being who resides behind the mask. There is indeed an "artistic" temperament at work. Fours like to be surrounded by beautiful things and to decorate their homes and apartments tastefully.

Fours are inveterate "romantics." The ups and downs of everyday life do not provide them with the intensity they seek. They have little urge "to blossom where they are planted." Rather, they tend to a fascination with the exotic, the far away, the fanciful and the adventurous. They can become withdrawn from the world in its concrete reality, withdrawn from the mundane circles in which "lesser folk" exist. As romantics, they are preoccupied with romantic love, too, and search after the ideal lover.

Unhealthy Fours tend to be snobs. The snob has a self-conscious sense of superiority, built upon an inner doubt as to his or her true worth. Fours, of course, have such doubts in plenty. In compensation, they may exhibit an over-refinement, a showy sensitivity, much of which is aimed at distancing themselves from lesser mortals. Not surprisingly, they often maintain a keen interest in social and class relationships, an interest that points up the concerns of an envious nature. It is in their envious mode, from behind their facade, that Fours observe others keenly—and then demean those others by belittling their humble concerns.

"Artists" by temperament, aware of the figurative and symbolic realm beneath the humdrum surface of things, Fours sometimes become artists in fact, translating their inner dramas into the productions of a poet or novelist, painter or sculptor. It is the self-

---

[37] *Ennea-Type Structures, Self-analysis for the Seeker,* pps. 69, 71

revealing side of the Four that prompts the creative effort. Through this side of their nature, they marshal a talent for self-expression. Their churning emotion is given shape and scope. The original work that ensues is a vital expression of themselves, deeply connected to their sense of worth. Thus the Four—the Four who is in fact an artist—comes to terms with himself or herself by creating a work of art that expresses the inner being in an outward manner.

To create—as well as to seek—the beautiful: To this the cultivated Four aspires. And to this aspiration there is more wisdom than less sensitive souls might think. In defense of the Four as dreamer, as seeker after will-o' the wisps, one might ponder the concept of *sehnsucht,* the German word for longing, nostalgia, deep yearning, "sweet melancholy." C. S. Lewis, in his *English Literature in the Sixteenth Century,* says that *sehnsucht* "would logically appear as among the sanest and most fruitful experiences we have," for the object of longing "really exists and really draws us to itself."[38] *Sehnsucht,* in this view, is a conduit of longing and desire for the "Other," for the Divine Being in whom one's restless heart may find rest. In this desire is a sort of "poetic proof" of divine reality. "Lewis makes clear his belief that a desire for God does support the idea of His existence."[39]

Introverts as well as individualists, Fours are at home in their inner universe, marching to the beat of their own drum. They see themselves as tragic, misunderstood figures, as entitled to inhabit—and to enjoy—a sub-world of sadness and loss, to which they have been driven by the cold, cruel world. In this they are like the Romantics of art and literature, proud and sensitive beings too good for this mortal coil, dwelling in twilight lands of impracticality and loss.

The Artist has in fact a deep discontent with his finiteness, with his limited nature, with his creatureliness. There is at work a deep rebellion, an unwillingness to admit one's humanness before the Creator. There is a desire to be the center of one's self-centered self, a desire to be autonomous. Yet these are desires whose satisfaction is

---

[38]Corbin Scott Carnell, *Bright Shadow of Reality: C. S. Lewis and the Feeling Intellect,* p. 137
[39]Carnell, p. 140

impossible, inasmuch as God alone is the only possible center for His human creatures. In rebelling thus, Fours refuse to love God enough to be contented, refuse to be thankful for the many gifts that He has given.

Owing to these traits and the unhappiness they bring, Fours can become self-hating, abusing themselves with drugs or unbridled sensuality. They may experience temporary pleasure from the pain and humiliation they inflict upon themselves, but their brooding thoughts and foolish actions ("A man's own folly ruins his life"— Proverbs 19:3) plunge them ever deeper into misery. In their lowest states, they watch the great parade of the world as it marches by, leaving them alone and undeveloped, looking on from the outside. In their isolation, they refuse the healing that could be got from confiding in a trusted friend, from appealing to God. Inasmuch as they see themselves as defective, as not "measuring up," they feel they should suffer.

With life at low ebb, the tragic sense of Fours comes into full play. Their sense of loss takes on dramatic form; they become lost souls, acting the part in all its aspects. Moods fluctuate even more than usual. Increasingly helpless, they seek someone to cling to. They hold onto relationships that are often frustrating, making an already bad situation worse. They may evoke the pity of others and may indeed be cared for, but they end up resenting their caretakers.

Joseph, favorite son of the Patriarch Jacob (Israel), bears the marks of a Four. He of the "richly ornamented robe" thought himself special and so did his father. Not surprisingly, the favoritism went to Joseph's head.

Joseph the dreamer was among life's intuitives. His dreams, dramatic in nature and clear in their message (they informed him that he was superior to his brothers and his father), were not only self-important but prophetic. Indeed, there would come a time when his family *would* bow before him. In the meantime, his siblings detested the dreamy loner who stayed at home while they grazed the flocks far away. When they got their chance, they stripped him, threw him in a cistern and sold him into slavery.

Joseph was taken to Egypt, where he was sold as a slave to Potiphar, captain of the guard. Despite his diligent and honorable service and the success it brought him, Joseph found himself falsely accused of making advances towards the mistress of the house. He was arrested but not abandoned; the Lord was with him. Joseph managed to thrive even in prison, where his dreams foretold the future yet again. Word of his gift reached Pharaoh, who asked him to interpret a dream. Joseph did so, explaining that it meant there would be seven years of plenty, followed by seven years of want. Joseph advised Pharaoh on how best to prepare for this circumstance. As a result, the Hebrew "outsider" was advanced to high office, where he served as Pharaoh's "vizier." By his policies in the years of plenty, he assured that everyone would have enough to eat in the years of famine—and he made Pharaoh rich in the bargain.

Joseph suffered but never lost faith. He trusted God to redeem him and He did. He governed Egypt wisely and, in the end, was reconciled to his brothers. When they abased themselves before him, before this man of dignity and power, he was reduced to tears. In the end he forgave them their sin against him. "You intended to harm me, but God intended it for good, to accomplish what is now being done, the saving of many lives" (Genesis 50:20). In this, Joseph spoke like an integrated Four, displaying the wisdom and the objectivity of a One, able to discern the ways of the Lord who had been with him in his many travails, always working for good.

A measure of "alienation" is necessary to moral renewal and spiritual progress. The heroes of scripture, the true heroes of any age, are to one degree or another (Joseph included) alienated from the culture of their day, from the imperatives of expediency, hedonism and materialism. Fours, perhaps more than any other type, are aware of the tensions inherent in alienation. Yet, owing to their sensitivity and insight, they will not, for good or ill, be found running with the herd. "I urge you, as aliens and strangers in the world, to abstain from sinful desires, which war against your soul" (1 Peter 2:11).

Alienation as alluded to here is not referenced in the pathological but the moral sense, as a sometimes necessary estrangement from self, others and one's surroundings. Such an estrangement is a necessity of self-consciousness, of maturity; it is the awareness by the sensitive soul of just how "out of joint" the world is, of how rife with corruption, conformity and cruelty. Should one make peace with such a world? Should one make peace with the people who *do* make peace with such a world? Indeed, should one make peace with one's self, a self complicit in the world's deeds? A measure of "healthy" alienation is required, towards self and others.[40]

Even so, Fours need to make common cause—albeit a *discerning* common cause—with others. They need, if they are believers, to take their place in the Body of Christ that is the church, and to learn that "the body is a unit, though it is made up of many parts; and though all its parts are many, they form one body" (1 Corinthians 12:12). They need to learn that "God has arranged the parts in the body, every one of them, just as he wanted them to be (vs 18)." God has made provision for his servants. He has set aside a place, prepared a path, designed a special task from all eternity. A part to be played awaits the Four, a part that will not smother the Four's creativity but one that will allow that creativity to achieve greater scope, to bear fruit. In this the Four is called to accept his or her finiteness, concrete circumstances and particular talent or talents. The Four is summoned to accept with gratitude his or her calling, rather than to pine continually for what never was and never will be.

The Four is encouraged to join the dance of life. "Always give yourselves fully to the work of the Lord, because you know that your labor in the Lord is not in vain" (1 Corinthians 15:58). There is vanity in standing on the sidelines, observing others, tittering at their mishaps, demeaning their motives—and envying their triumphs. The Four needs to open up to the ordinary, to get his hands dirty in a good cause, to recognize that God—even God—has submitted to the narrow confines of human life. God Himself, in the person of Jesus Christ, took on the narrow, ordinary life that all human beings live, took on the task of dying, dying a death worse than his followers will ever have to endure. The finiteness and mortality of the human condition have been shared to the full by Deity Himself.

---

[40] The matter is discussed at length in Walter Kaufmann's *From Decidophobia to Autonomy: Without Guilt and Justice,* pps. 140-147

The Four is advised to divert the uncontrolled emotions that can spiral him into sin. He or she needs to harness these emotions, to transmute them into good work and good works and to avoid the pitfalls of melancholy. The Four must not dream only but must *do.* It takes work to be happy, effort to be fulfilled. God is happy to cooperate; He has work for everyone, a place for everyone, in the spiritual battle. "What makes life worth while is having a big enough objective, something which catches our imagination and lays hold of our allegiance; and this the Christian has, in a way that no other man has."[41]

As in the Parable of the Talents, the single talent should not be buried but well employed. In the case of the Four, there may be additional talents, as well, and they need to be employed, too. "Do not merely listen to the word, and so deceive yourselves. Do what it says" (James 1:22). The dreamy Four is to become more objective, to become more goal-oriented, to become more "earthy," even while retaining the deep and profound longings so characteristic of the type. "The solid wisdom for man or boy who is haunted with the hovering of unseen wings, with the scent of unseen roses, and the subtle enticements of 'melodies unheard,' is *work.* If he follow any of those, they will vanish. But if he work, they will come unsought."[42]

Prone to melancholy, Fours fear especially the final enemy, death, and brood upon that enemy, aware that this natural world is "ever passing." The Four is therefore wise to accept the inevitable, to face the facts, but to face them with faith; to learn to trust in that which overcomes death. "Blessed are those who mourn, for they will be comforted" (Matthew 5:4). The Four must recollect in times of trial that "those who suffer he delivers in their suffering; he speaks to them in their affliction" (Job 36:15). Further, that "the Father of compassion... comforts us in all our troubles so that we can comfort those in any trouble with the comfort we ourselves have received from God" (1 Corinthians 1:3-4).

The Four need not suppress his or her emotions but needs to regulate them, to combine achievement and art, work and wistful

---

[41] J. I. Packer, *Knowing God,* p. 30
[42] C. S. Lewis, *George MacDonald, An Anthology,* p. 109

nostalgia, dream and reality. God is no stoic, nor should his people be. Scripture teaches that God feels joy, sorrow, delight, love—and even fear. The incarnate Second Person of God, Jesus of Nazareth, certainly suffered the most acute anxiety in the garden, where he sweated drops of blood. "Father, if you are willing, take this cup from me" (Luke 22:42).

The Four must be ready, like Jesus, to drink of the cup, to offer willing service to God, in spite of anguish in the face of fear. The Four must learn also to ask, with Paul, in ever deepening faith: "Where, O death, is your victory? Where, O death, is your sting?" (1 Corinthians 15:55), and to echo with Paul the triumphant answer: "When the perishable has been clothed with the imperishable, and the mortal with immortality, then the saying that is written will come true: 'Death has been swallowed up in victory'" (vs 54).

The Four who is a justified sinner needs to remind himself that he has been "buried with Christ" in baptism, that he is "dead to sin," that he will be raised with Christ; indeed, that he is raised daily in a foretaste of the heavenly things to come. There is a pattern of death and rebirth in all his days and to the end of his days. Thereafter follows glory.

Ole Hallesby, a profound student of character, saw deeply into the melancholic temperament, empathizing and offering hope, underscoring a conviction that those who are more sensitive, inner-directed and imaginative may be deserving of the greatest honors. His words are pertinent to the Four: "No one but a melancholic can appreciate fully the sufferings the melancholic must undergo. But remember, dear friends: The disciple whom the Lord loved was a melancholic man."[43]

---

[43] *Temperament and the Christian Faith,* p. 59

6

The Thinker

"The mind cannot long act the role of the heart."
—La Rochefoucauld

The Five, the "Thinker," is found in the Triad of the Mind. The number of this type "is significant of Divine strength added to and made perfect in... weakness; of omnipotence combined with the impotence of earth; of Divine *favour* uninfluenced and invincible."[44] Fives, dwelling within their heads and wary of the outside world, do indeed bear a measure of "weakness" and "impotence"—in spite of a strong and independent mind—that only God's favour can overcome.

The capital sin of the type is greed or "avarice." The avarice is not so much for worldly goods as it is to know things, to know *everything*. The greed to know stems from a fear of the world "out there" and the need to counter that fear. Fives, C. G. Jung's *introverted thinking type,* blunt the threat by amassing knowledge and piling up theories, ideas and concepts. By storing up knowledge, they hope to become self-reliant and safe, comprehending but keeping at arm's length the ever-threatening world.

Fives, clear-headed and little given to wishful thinking, are keen observers. Combined with their ability to think abstractly, this faculty

---

[44] Bullinger, *Number in Scripture,* p. 135

can turn them into scholars, intellectuals, researchers and analysts. They are always scanning people and places. They don't miss a thing. They evaluate and store the reams of data that pour in.

They are non-judgmental; they simply want to know, to watch the passing scene and take it in even as they hide from it. What they observe they think upon. Yet the role of observer, played out at the expense of a more rounded lifestyle, can develop in them an imbalance between thought and action. Even as their minds are active, their emotions are bottled up. They can appear "uptight," restrained in movement and posture, absent-minded.

In addition, Fives can feel misunderstood. After all, who can rise to their level of understanding? Who is worthy to share their thoughts? Unlike St. Paul, they do not feel "obligated both to the wise and the foolish" (Romans 1:14). The wise—or at least the brainy—are enough for them, thank you. Thus they become isolated and anti-social.

Thinkers, at times nearly overwhelmed by hypersensitivity, are withdrawing types. They attempt to keep out the instrusions of the world, the better to defend themselves, although sensitivity to pain and noise remains. Their solitude can, in excess, open them to inner dangers, inner "demons," to "the Devil, who ever consorts with our solitude."[45]

Some of the threats the Five perceives are, of course, real. The world is a dangerous place. By and large, however, "projection" (ascribing their own thoughts and feelings to others) is the source of their fear. They read hidden dangers into the innocent remarks and actions of others, or into random things that happen in the everyday world.

Unhealthy Thinkers, living on the inside and making little mark on the outside world, come to feel powerless, unable to act naturally and appropriately. They become increasingly fearful as they withdraw from the challenges of daily living. Instead of learning life skills in the real world, they become more and more preoccupied with their interior lives. Their spinning of theories and fantasies leaves them at a loss in dealing with outer realities. They become all "head," no emotion or instinct. "The main picture that emerges... is that of a

---

[45] Sir Thomas Browne

person who holds himself down to the extent of shriveling in stature, in order to avoid expansive moves."[46]

The Five's characteristic form of fear is anxiety, a diffuse feeling of dread. This is a feeling fed by unconscious impulses and conflicts. They suffer uneasiness, a lurking fear of catastrophy. By taking thought, they hope to keep this menace at bay. By acquiring and ordering a mass of knowledge, they hope to inject an element of predictability into day-to-day living, to outwit the dangers that threaten.

Greed, or avarice, the significant fault of the Five, is one of the "seven deadly sins" or capital sins. As indicated above, Fives are not greedy in a materialistic sense. They are not greedy for power or prestige or great wealth, as Eights or Threes or other types can be. They are, rather, greedy for knowledge. Yet, in addition to their appetite for knowledge, they can be "tight-fisted," stingy with their time, money, emotions, possessions, thoughts and discoveries. They want to keep it all to themselves, the better to keep themselves safe from the intruding world. To live in this way, they reduce their needs and hoard their resources, making themselves less dependent on others.

Thinkers tend to be aloof, bored with small talk. They are ill at ease with social niceties and humdrum activities. Often socially awkward, they find attendance at public functions burdensome. They do not like the shallow chatter or "pointless" activities of a group. They can be, like the introverted thinking type they resemble, "gauche in ... behavior, painfully anxious to escape notice, or else remarkably unconcerned and childishly naive."[47] While others maintain a buzz of conversation, Fives keep their feelings to themselves and frequently lapse into silence. ("This type tends to vanish behind a cloud of misunderstanding.")[48]

Similarly, they do not like reaching out to others, let alone making a commitment to them. They prefer time to themselves. In their "cave," they can assess the facts and theories that fill their minds, an activity

---

[46] Karen Horney, *Neurosis and Human Growth, The Struggle Toward Self-Realization,* p. 221
[47] Jung, *Psychological Types,* p. 385
[48] Ibid., p. 384

that avoids the hazards of personal contact. Conseqently, they resent intrusions. Their home is their castle.

Owing to their absent-mindedness, Thinkers maintain only a superficial connection to everyday physical reality. They are not at home in the body. The world of the senses remains unexplored, all the better to avoid the dangers of the physical world. Hence the tendency to clumsiness and the preference for thinking over doing.

As an individualist, outsider and loner, the Five tends to be detached from the customary views of the larger society. This isolation can lead to aggression against the beliefs and opinions of others. Fives prefer to build their own theories, to form their own opinions. "Knowledge puffeth up" but the Five revels in knowledge, even as he or she disdains the common run of humanity.

Owing to their detachment and social indifference, Fives may develop a wry sense of humor. Their breadth of knowledge, coupled with keen observation, provides the means to pierce social pretense or see humor in a situation from an unexpected angle. Reserved though they are, Fives may burst into laughter at such moments, catching others off guard and amusing the crowd—and themselves.

As they slip into unhealthy states, Fives become increasingly stubborn. They refuse the helpful suggestions of others, they avoid playing anyone else's "game." Their minds, working overtime, take on a life of their own, becoming "overheated" as it were. Darker forces can be at work, too: "His head is like a thought machine," observes Watchman Nee (in a passage that brings to mind the deteriorating Five), "operated by external force; it continues to think but is impotent to desist. ... the thoughts in his mind... come to him in waves, rolling unceasingly day and night. There is no way to terminate them. He is not aware that this is but the activity of the evil spirit... in the case of these unmanageable thoughts it is not that his mind is grasping at something but rather that something is grasping his mind. In the natural course of events it is the mind which thinks about matters; now it is these matters which force the mind to think."[49]

Fives, in spiraling downwards, become cynical, distrusting selfless acts and disinterested points of view. They are suspicious of the face

---

[49]*The Spiritual Man,* Vol. 3, p. 15

value of persons and situations, always suspecting a hidden agenda. They reject laws and institutions, become skeptical, and think themselves smart enough to see through everything. Thus they preserve their independence—and isolation. Neither God, man nor tradition has a claim on them. They "quench the Spirit" and their life becomes ever more empty.

Ultimately, the Thinkers' strategy fails because the underlying problem goes deeper than he or she is aware of. The problem is more than free-floating fear, attached first to this and then to that. The problem, at bottom, is an inner sense of "nothingness," a sense projected onto the outer world. Fives, in their probing thoughts, grasp the possibility of non-being, of an absence of all that is good and worthwhile.

The Apostle Thomas bears the pattern of a Five. The name that tradition has given him, "Doubting Thomas," points to an element of skepticism in his nature. "Unless I see the nail marks in his hands and put my finger where the nails were, and put my hand into his side, I will not believe it." Thomas, who uttered these words, had been absent (how like a Five) when the Resurrected Jesus had appeared to the rest of the disciples. When he was told the remarkable news, Thomas expressed doubt. Even though he had been with Jesus when the master had performed miracles and wonders, he could not bring himself to believe in this, the greatest of miracles.

Why such doubt? Why, that is, beyond the instrinsic unlikelihood of such a stupendous event as the Resurrection? (But should it have been unlikely in view of earlier events? After all, the disciples had seen Jesus raise the dead on more than one occasion). One could surmise the reason for Thomas's doubt was bitter disappointment, laced with his inherent skepticism.* After all, Thomas had shared the joy and excitement of "Palm Sunday," as he had experienced the heady, triumphal entry into Jerusalem. Then, days later, he had been plunged into despair by the events of the Passion. As a result, everything appeared lost. Thomas, stressed and numbed, had hoped in vain. So he chose to retreat to his own lonely center, to rely on his own resources. To do this he had to wilfully say "no" to reports of the

Resurrection, to put the whole business out of his mind, once for all. The outer world—the world with all of its pain and disappointment and death—would not be allowed to dash his hopes again. He had suffered enough.

Eight days later, Jesus returned. Thomas was summoned. Jesus offered tangible evidence to his skeptical follower: "Put your finger here; see my hands. Reach out your hand and put it into my side. Stop doubting and believe." Thomas was overwhelmed, his defenses breached. In an instant, he was transformed. "My Lord and my God!" He had been offered proof of the Resurrection, the proof of the senses (and something more, no doubt; the overwhelming authority, personality and "presence" of Jesus). This grace was possible to contemporaries of Jesus' days on earth, to such as Thomas. To the many generations that have followed, belief has been mediated by the Word and the Spirit through faith. "Because you have seen me," Jesus said to Thomas, "you have believed; blessed are those who have not seen and yet have believed." Blessed *indeed* are they who believe in these latter days, be they Fives or any other type.

A fine portrait of another Five, highlighting additional aspects of the type, is presented in *The Varieties of Religious Experience,* wherein the skimping, minimizing (but in this case rather saintly) traits of the type are evident. According to a memoir of the Unitarian minister and writer, William Ellery Channing, the young clergyman:

> "... seemed to have become incapable of any form of self-indulgence. He took the smallest room in the house for his study, though he might easily have commanded one more light, airy, and in every way more suitable; and chose for his sleeping chamber an attic which he shared with a younger brother. The furniture of the latter might have answered for the cell of an anchorite, and consisted of a hard mattress on a cot-bedstead, plain wooden chairs and table, with matting on the floor. It was without fire, and so cold he was throughout life extremely sensitive; but he never complained or appeared in any way to be conscious of inconvenience. 'I recollect,' says his brother, 'after one most severe night, that in the morning

he sportively thus alluded to his suffering: 'If my bed were my country, I should be somewhat like Bonaparte: I have no control except over the part which I occupy; the instant I move, frost takes possession.' In sickness only would he change for the time his apartment and accept a few comforts. The dress too that he habitually adopted was of most inferior quality; and garments were constantly worn which the world would call mean."[50]

At healthy levels of personality, Thinkers are busy with useful projects and ideas, thereby contributing something worthwhile to the world of which they are part. Even when healthy, they are marked by characteristic traits. In the workplace, for instance, they are at their best when left alone, as they resent close supervision. The boss, if smart, will discover that the Five "is best put in a room alone and allowed to play"—the better to tap the creative juices of this aloof type. Once motivated Fives are unstoppable in pursuit of their goal. They are innovators, problem-solvers, eager to break new ground. But when a project is completed, they are ready to move on to new challenges.

At their best, Fives can be bold thinkers, devising complex theories to interpret and order disparate facts in novel ways. They can turn an avalanche of data into a coherent whole. They synthesize unlikely ideas, observing connections that others have missed. They seek patterns and deeper meanings beyond the obvious. They may develop a predictive ability, "prophetic" in a natural sense, discerning the likely outcome of events. Such insight into how things fit together and why they behave the way they do can lead to an increased understanding of other people, too, creating a much-needed link to the rest of humanity.

The Thinker needs to put the life of the mind in perspective rather than abandon it, and to open himself or herself to engagement with other persons and the world around. "Of making many books there is no end, and much study wearies the body" (Ecclesiastes 12:12). The

---

[50] William James, pps. 300-301

windows of the soul need to be thrown open to the fresh breezes of the Spirit.

Fives need to honestly search out the Divine. They need to ask, seek and knock with the hope they will be answered, that they will find, and that the door will be opened. "And without faith it is impossible to please God, because anyone who comes to him must believe that he exists and that he rewards those who earnestly seek him" (Hebrews 11:6). They need to step out into life like Peter into the sea, knowing the Saviour will come to the rescue when doubt pulls them beneath the turbulent waves.

The independently-minded Five needs to learn that he or she is a creature encircled by the divine reality in which, as St. Paul says, human beings live and move and have their being. No man is an island, no human being is cut off from the Source of being. "Who endowed the heart with wisdom," God asks Job, "or gave understanding to the mind?" (36:38). Fives did not create their being, nor their understanding, nor the universe in which they dwell. A woodsman cannot cut off the limb upon which he sits and expect to remain connected to the tree; no more can a Five sever his being from the root of all being and expect to be nourished. A direct, living relationship is required. "Experimental knowledge of the truth as revealed to the heart of the individual directly by the Father is the only possible key to the kingdom of God."[51]

Thinkers need to learn that "real life" experience, painful though it may be, is as great a teacher as the pages of a book. And they need to know that in facing the fears of life they do not face them alone. "Cast all your anxiety on him because he cares for you" (1 Peter 5:7). The passion for piling up facts and ideas and theories needs to be tamed.

The Five, a potential fountain of wisdom, needs to discharge the tightly packed contents and energies of the inner life into the world around, there to benefit others and bring himself into balance. This can be done by learning the difference between knowledge—in the sense of facts and theories—and wisdom, with its power to discern and judge what is true or right. "He who gets wisdom loves his own

---

[51] E. Y. Mullens, *The Axioms of Religion,* p. 95

soul; he who cherishes understanding prospers" (Proverbs 19:8).

The Five's bent for being miserly with the goods of the creation as well as the goods of the mind runs everywhere counter to scripture. Jesus makes it clear in the Sermon on the Mount that his followers are "not to store up for [themselves] treasures on earth, where moth and rust destroy, and where thieves break in and steal" (Matthew 6:19). How much better and wiser to be generous with one's possessions. Paul, in his turn, adduces a principle concerning generosity: "Remember this: Whoever sows sparingly will also reap sparingly, and whoever sows generously will also reap generously" (2 Corinthians 9:6). The Old Testament is equally pointed: "Do not withhold good from those who deserve it when it is in your power to act" (Proverbs 3:27). Another Proverb points up the enlightened self-interest of the generous: "One man gives freely, yet gains even more; another withholds unduly, but comes to poverty. A generous man will prosper; he who refreshes others will himself be refreshed" (Proverbs 11:24-25).

Thinkers, in becoming more balanced, need to be reminded of their bond with God and the community of believers. "Don't you know that you yourselves are God's temple, and that God's Spirit lives in you?" (1 Corinthians 3:16). They need to see themselves as parts of the Body of Christ; as dependent, not isolated beings. As the writer to the Hebrews urges: "And let us consider how we may spur one another on toward love and good deeds. Let us not give up meeting together as some are in the habit of doing, but let us encourage one another" (Hebrews 10:24-25). Even the Five—that withdrawing individualist—has a place in the Body and is a beneficiary of the Body's wisdom. "For where two or three come together in my name, there am I with them" (Matthew 18:20).

Ever increasing knowledge—by itself—will never satisfy the heart of the Five, nor will it provide protection from social realities and natural calamities. Neither will the Five's own thoughts, no matter how clever and complex, calm the anxieties within. Even knowledge of the Divine, apart from "heart" knowledge, love and obedience, will prove unhelpful. "For although they knew God, they neither glorified him as God nor gave thanks to him, but their thinking became futile and their foolish hearts were darkened" (Romans 1:21). To be futile in one's thinking, to remain isolated in one's head, to remain outside the divine relationship, is to remain unfulfilled. A living relationship to the Divine is essential. The word of Christ "is not an abstract doctrine, but the re-creation of the whole life of man... The call to follow implies that there is only one way of believing on Jesus Christ, and that is by leaving all and going with the incarnate Son of God."[52]

Such a relationship awaits the humble seeker, the seeker who brings nothing with him or her but seeks only the grace of God by faith. The proper order is faith first, then understanding. ("Faith, not reason, is the basis of Christian knowledge."—Karl Barth). This the healthy Thinker realizes. Only God can quench the thirst of the spirit; only God, not endless thought, will bring true knowledge. "For as he thinketh in his heart, so is he" (Proverbs 23:7).

* As suggested in the chapter, "Hope When I Find It Hard to Believe," in *Never Beyond Hope: How God Touches and Uses Imperfect People,* by J. I. Packer and Carolyn Nystrom.

---

[52] Dietrich Bonhoeffer, *The Cost of Discipleship,* p. 67

7

The Guardian

"Two souls, alas, within me sink and surge. Each would
be riven from its brother."
—Goethe, *Faust*

Sixes are "all too human."

In fact, Six "is the number of imperfection; the human number; the number of MAN as destitute of God, without God, without Christ... *man* was created on the *sixth* day, and thus he has the number *six* impressed upon him... *Six,* therefore, is the number of *labour*... of man's labour as apart and distinct from God's rest."[53]

Everyone is fearful at times and some types are beset by a higher than normal amount of fear (the Five for instance). Guardians, however, have a special problem with fear. They are not only fearful but *aware* of being fearful.

Located in the center of the Triad of the Mind, they are plagued by anxiety, a free-floating fear that overlays daily experience. As "worry warts," they are vividly aware of all the things that can go wrong. And as professional worriers, they develop stratagems to curb their worries. For instance, they engage in "magical thinking," believing their worst fears will fail to materialize because they have already "experienced" them in a hundred lurid imaginings.

Detached from "God's rest," Sixes are not only fearful of real (and imagined) threats but doubtful of their abilities and afraid of

---

[53] Bullinger, *Number in Scripture,* p. 150

being alone and disliked. Feeling "destitute of God," they find their ultimate authority on the human plane. They are ready and willing to do what the human authority expects of them, a strategy that ensures (they think) safety. Thus Guardians avoid violating "the norm" and identify with those who represent recognized standards. Aware of their own temptations to deviate from the customary, they project those temptations onto others—and then judge those others harshly.

Though excessively dutiful, Sixes distrust other people. And why not? They distrust themselves, after all. Again, it's a matter of projection, of seeing themselves in others. As a result, they would rather be subject to impersonal and rigid rules than to the less predictable qualities of personal relationships. Security trumps intimacy with others.

Sixes, in striving to do good things and to do them right, are beset by performance anxieties. When seeking approval, they live in fear of mistakes, large and small. They repeat themselves again and again ("Is it okay? Shall we move ahead, then?") to ensure acceptance of their suggestions and decisions.

Guardians can be "clubby" and engaging, loyal to the church, the party, the company. Their "naive, spontaneous, genial nature opens doors and hearts." (Ole Hallesby, speaking of "sanguines," elements of which are found in the Six). They can be charming and disarming, with a talent for hospitality. They are quick to criticize or minimize themselves, not only to make others feel at ease but to short-circuit criticism. "Sorry, I just threw this together at the last minute. I hope you like it." Dare anyone object?

To remain in their comfort zone, Guardians tend to view issues as black or white. Inconvenient facts that might disturb their cherished beliefs are ignored. In all things, tradition rules. They are wary of change and so cultivate conservatism. When questions arise about the course to follow, they want to know how things were done in the past. This avoids breaking new ground, reduces the need for choice and allays anxiety. When they find themselves puzzled, they redouble their efforts to tidy up the system. They are skilled at interpreting every jot and tittle of the rules and thereby forestall the anxiety caused by uncertainty.

Sixes find it hard to initiate projects. They become hesitant, tentative. They lack confidence. Even a course of action that appears do-able stirs fear, fear that the status quo may be altered. "Better the devil you know..." Thus they are held back by an inner resistance; they develop a talent for postponing their lives.

Despite their fears, Guardians are not "wimps." Timid when out of their element, they can become tough and stubborn within a well-defined setting, especially when they are in charge of a situation. Unyielding and defensive, they can be threatening in the name of the in-group. They see through the eyes of "their own kind" and "group think" is a guiding principle. They can turn into bullies, sparing others as little as they have spared themselves.

Further, in attempting to counter their sense of fear, they can act in ways opposite their normal inclinations ("counterphobia"). They may take surprising risks, back-talking the boss or doing a bungee-jump, all in the hope of putting their nagging anxieties out of mind.

The Six is related to C. G. Jung's *Introverted Feeling Type*. According to Jung, the type consists principally of women, a view that is not shared by Enneagram theory. His words on the type, however, are interesting, especially as he brings out the suspicious and combative nature of less than healthy members of the type. Accordingly, the *Introverted Feeling Type* suspects others "are thinking all sorts of mean things, scheming evil, contriving plots, secret intrigues, etc. In order to forestall them, she herself is obliged to start counter-intrigues, to suspect others and sound them out, and weave counterplots... Endless clandestine rivalries spring up, and in these embittered struggles she will shrink from no baseness or meanness, and will even prostitute her virtues in order to play the trump card."[54]

Skilled at seeing their inner faults—faults that are generally undetectable by others—Sixes find it hard to accept at face value the praises they receive. Owing to this self-opposition, their self-esteem is at the mercy of others. Thus they feel pressured and strive to do the "right thing." Consequently they work even harder to keep the rules and follow the right course. In doing so, they add to their anxieties.

---

[54] *Psychological Types,* p. 391

Sixes, who are "head types," can have a philosophical turn of mind. They see, despite their attraction to authority, the pros and cons of an issue. Their self-doubts and endless inner questioning tend to hone their skills in logic. Reaching as they do for absolutes, they add the passion of the "true believer" to their quiver of arrows.

Above everything else, Sixes are ambivalent, torn between fear and counter-fear. They are filled with contradictions, swinging pendulum-like from one pole to the other. They strongly support authority and are submissive to it, yet frequently fear and resent it. They obey... yet secretly wish to rebel. Traditionalists to the core, they weary of tradition. They chafe under external restraints. They long for security but take foolish risks. Their anxieties impel them first one way, then another; at one moment towards dependence and the next towards defiance.

A genteel expression of "the divided self" (in the phrase of William James) can be found in the words of Annie Besant, the English Theosophist:

> I have ever been the queerest mixture of weakness and strength, and have paid heavily for the weakness. As a child I used to suffer tortures of shyness, and if my shoe-lace was untied would feel shamefacedly that every eye was fixed on the unlucky string; as a girl I would shrink away from strangers and think myself unwanted and unliked, so that I was full of eager gratitude to any one who noticed me kindly; as the young mistress of a house I was afraid of my servants, and would let careless work pass rather than bear the pain of reproving the ill-doer; when I have been lecturing and debating with no lack of spirit on the platform, I have preferred to go without what I wanted at the hotel rather than to ring and make the waiter fetch it. Combative on the platform in defense of any cause I cared for, I shrink from quarrel or disapproval in the house, and am a coward at heart in private while a good fighter in public. How often have I passed unhappy quarters of an hour screwing up my courage to find fault with some subordinate whom my duty compelled me to reprove, and how often have I jeered at myself for a fraud as the doughty

platform combatant, when shrinking from blaming some lad or lass for doing their work badly. An unkind look or word has availed to make me shrink into myself as a snail into its shell, while, on the platform, opposition makes me speak my best.[55]

In sum, the Six is a conflicted individual, loyal but defiant, rulebound but rebellious. Yet the Six can be, when healthy, an impressive figure. The healthy Six excels at being affectionate, dependable, loyal. Sixes are team players, willing to soldier along for the good of the cause and of the people with whom they are aligned. They learn to trust themselves and others and to affirm, instead of negate, their gifts. They can learn to laugh at their fears and make decisions for themselves, instead of relying on the authority of others.

In the Apostle Peter, one finds an inconsistent Six, phobic (fearful) and counterphobic by turns. Alexander Whyte captures the apostle's sanguine traits: "The worst disease of the human heart is cold," he writes. "Well, with all his [Peter's] faults, and he was full of them, a cold heart was not one of them. All Peter's faults, indeed, lay in the heat of his heart. He was too hot-hearted, too impulsive, too enthusiastic. His hot heart was always in his mouth, and he spoke it all out many times when he should have held his peace."[56]

Such was the counterphobic Peter. Quick to act, aggressive, gifted with leadership abilities, Peter was a man of courage and conviction. At the time of Jesus' arrest in the garden, he drew his sword and cut off the ear of Malchus, a member of the arresting party. Though told to sheathe his sword by Jesus, he had shown a willingness to fight for his master. Earlier, he had made it known (embarrassingly, it turns out) that he was willing to die rather than disown Jesus. In Acts, he preached the Spirit-empowered sermon on Pentecost. Later, he defied the Jewish high council, expressing keenness to obey God rather than men, regardless of cost.

---

[55] Besant, *Autobiography,* quoted by William James, *The Varieties of Religious Experience,* pps. 168-169

[56] Tim LaHaye, *Transformed Temperaments,* p. 38, quoting from *Treasury of Alexander Whyte*

Peter: a loyalist, a team player, a Guardian and, on one occasion, a judgmental enforcer of the rules. Devoted to his master, he tried (wrong-headedly) to dissuade Jesus from his path of suffering. Throughout the Gospels, he gravitated toward leadership but did not usurp power. Later, in Acts, he displayed fierce indignation in the judgment of Ananias and Sapphira.

The phobic side of Peter is evident, as well. After proclaiming his loyalty unto death, Peter disowned Jesus three times, an act of cowardice that was predicted by the master. Peter showed weakness of character in a later incident, too, when he backed down from fear before the Judaizers (those who believed that circumscision was necessary for salvation).

The Bible puts fear in perspective.

In its well known words, Proverbs 1:7 lays the foundation: "The fear of the LORD is the beginning of knowledge, but fools despise wisdom and discipline." This speaks of the one "fear" that can subdue all other fears. "Fear of the LORD" does not mean a cringing timidity but rather a reverence of and submission to a Lord who loves his people, every one of them. By learning to place more and more of their fears within the circle of Him "in whom we live and move and have our being," Sixes can defuse the fears over which they customarily obsess.

Isaiah's words affirm God's caring and supportive intentions: "You will keep in perfect peace him whose mind is steadfast, because he trusts in you" (26:3). How a Six yearns for that peace! And, "Do not fear, for I am with you; I will strengthen you and help you; I will uphold you with my righteous right hand" (41:10). The Lord can be relied on to counter the afflictions of an anxious mind. With His "right hand," the hand of power and salvation, He is utterly trustworthy. The mind that finds rest by trusting in the Lord becomes "steadfast," not plagued by fear and self-doubt.

Sixes are encouraged by Jesus to lessen their fears by setting proper priorities and focusing on the present. In the Sermon on the Mount, He addresses those who belabor the countless "what-ifs" of life. "But seek first his kingdom and his righteousness, and all these things [food, drink, clothing and the other necessities] will be given to you as well. Therefore do not worry about tomorrow; for tomorrow will worry about itself. Each day has enough trouble of its own" (Matthew 6:33-34). Worry will not solve tomorrow's problems; better to address today's concerns, about which one can do something. By facing problems head-on in the here-and-now one not only solves them (perhaps) but defuses the worries they cause. Avoiding problems only heightens fear and puts off the moment of reckoning.

Further, Sixes need to raise in prayer "the empty hands of faith." A life of prayer, of sincere and personal communication with God, a disciplined centering in the Divine, can go far in easing the anxieties that plague the soul. Sixes are well advised to maintain an open conduit to God. The Apostle Paul has it right: "Do not be anxious about anything, but in everything, by prayer and petition, with thanksgiving [how important that "thanksgiving" is], present your requests to God. And the peace of God, which transcends all understanding, will guard your hearts and your minds in Christ Jesus" (Philippians 4:6-7). Prayer, an intimate relationship with God, and petition, the boldness to present one's requests to God, are two of three keys to maintaining a spiritual and psychological balance.

"Thanksgiving" is the third. One who counts his or her blessings will discover much to be grateful for. The peace thus attained "transcends;" it goes "above and beyond," surpassing human understanding. "For you did not receive a Spirit that makes you a slave again to fear" (Romans 8:15). It is not a "psychological peace," a peace centered in the human faculties. Rather, it is a spiritual peace, a peace that can only be known when the believer realizes his sins are forgiven and that he can cast all his cares on the Lord.

However, prayer is not a magic formula. It does not always "work." One does not always receive that for which one asks. Yet "unanswered" prayer can be God's means of sanctifying a believer, of building patience and courage. Anxiety may continue to disturb, yet there is room for hope. Even here, one can find a silver lining. "Some people feel guilty about their anxieties and regard them as a defect of faith. I don't agree at all. They are afflictions, not sins. Like all afflictions, they are, if we can so take them, our share in the Passion of Christ."[57]

In Christian tradition, the obedience and dutifulness of Sixes are virtues. "Everyone must submit himself to the governing authorities, for there is no authority except that which God has established" (Romans 13:1). However, these virtues can be put to unworthy uses. It is one thing to be an obedient and useful citizen in civil society, another to be enslaved to the petty rules and rituals of pharisaical religion. The Six must be alert to the danger. The personal must not be sacrificed willy-nilly to dubious authority, in matters of civil life or in matters of faith. "A religion which commands awakens revolt, if there are only commands. Christianity as a personal religion begins with faith. Its method of growth is fellowship with God, entering into his plans, grasping his aims."[58]

Jesus overturns the values that motivate the generality of men and women. Humility, not pride, is central. "You are not to be called 'Rabbi,'" Jesus says, "for you have only one Master and you are all brothers. And do not call anyone on earth 'father,' for you have one Father, and he is in heaven. Nor are you to be called 'teacher,' for you have one Teacher, the Christ. The greatest among you will be your servant. For whoever exalts himself will be humbled and whoever humbles himself will be exalted" (Matthew 23:8-12). The greatest of Christ's followers are to be "servants," the very role a healthy Six can play in a gifted manner. Good servants make good leaders and vice versa. The unhealthy Six, by contrast, serves the powerful while turning on others.

Owing to a changed heart and energized by the Holy Spirit, Sixes thus learn to serve—and live—rightly. The fetters of misinterpreted and rigidified law are loosened. They find "their attempts at obedience are now joyful, integrated in a way that was never true before. Sin rules them no longer. In this respect, too, they have been liberated from bondage."[59] Imperfect still (and who isn't?), they are freer, lighter, more joyful. Obedience—hitherto a heavy bondage—becomes at last a light burden, an easy yoke.

---

[57] C. S. Lewis, *Letters to Malcolm, Chiefly on Prayer,* p. 41
[58] E. Y. Mullens, *The Axioms of Religion,* pp 28-29
[59] J. I. Packer, *Concise Theology,* pps. 173-174

Above all, the Six develops independence of mind and a healthy self-reliance, even while—paradoxically—relying more fully on God. "But the first and finest expression of Christ's lordship over the individual believer is in the gift of autonomy to him. Christ discovers each man to himself and starts him on an autonomous career, but never for a moment does he relax his grasp upon that man's conscience or life. Yet nothing thrills men into such a sense of freedom and power."[60]

Christ makes his followers "kings and priests unto God," releasing them from the bondage of a fearful self, freeing and empowering them for a fuller life. They are free at last and free to serve.

---

[60] Mullens, *Axioms,* p. 128

8

The Adventurer

"Nothing is so insufferable to man as to be completely at
rest, without passions, without business, without diversions,
without study. He then feels his nothingness,
his forlornness, his insufficiency, his dependence, his
weakness, and his emptiness. There will immmediately
arise from the depth of his heart weariness,
gloom, sadness, fretfulness, vexation."
—Blaise Pascal

Seven is from the root word *savah, "to be full or satisfied, have enough of.* Hence the meaning of the word 'seven' is dominated by this root, for on the *seventh* day God rested from the work of Creation."[61]

These elements get to the heart of the Seven, or "Adventurer." For here is a type that combines a never-ending quest to "be full or satisfied" and an inability to find satisfaction or "rest" amidst the creation that surrounds him.

Adventurers are enslaved to gluttony, one of the seven capital sins of Christian tradition. Owing to this root sin, Sevens pursue pleasure, experience and adventure. They are the ultimate consumers, ever in search of the finest foods, the trendiest clothes, the latest hobbies, the current "in" places. Sensuous and sensual, they are like

---

[61] Bullinger, *Number in Scripture,* pp. 167-68

the "pagans" whom Jesus cites in Matthew 6:31-32: "So do not worry, saying 'What shall we eat?' or 'What shall we drink' or 'What shall we wear?' For the pagans run after all these things."

So does the Seven. And Sevens do it to ease the anxieties of their souls. Their urges, conflicts and fantasies are translated into uncontrolled and generally undigested action.

The Seven personality is nothing new in the annals of humankind. In speaking of a related type in the tradition of Galen, C. S. Lewis observes that "The Sanguine man is plump, cheerful and hopeful. A fifteenth-century manuscript symbolises this complexion by a man and a woman, richly dressed, playing on stringed instruments on a flowery place."[62]

Adventurers are found in the Triad of the Mind, next to the "doing" or "gut" triad. A "head" type, the Seven is an extrovert who uses his mind to avoid pain at all cost. In doing so, Sevens often "leap before they look." Focused in the moment, living in the here and now, they see the trees but not the forest. Loveable and laughable one minute, they are exasperating the next. Erratic behavior is a troublesome characteristic, as the consequences of their actions appear distantly unreal.

Sevens seek with gusto the things they want, even as they hold at arm's length the serious questions they hesitate to ask. In keeping busy, they tend to "bite off more than they can chew," thus protecting themselves from brooding on life's unpleasant realities. They are averse to self-examination. ("Who, me worry?"). They are also short on follow through, tending to leave a trail of unfinished projects in their wake. They would—if they could slow down long enough to read it—resonate to Willem van Wulfen's *The Sybarite: A Guide to the Ruthless Enjoyment of Life.*

Sevens fit the image of the Yuppie who is in thrall to the latest fashions in apparel, electronics and travel. In pursuit of the world's goods, they turn their face from the painful realities that might temper their indulgence. In this, the Seven is like the "light-blooded" type who "is carefree and full of expectation; he attributes great importance

---

[62] *The Discarded Image, An Introduction to Medieval and Renaissance Literature*, p. 171

to everything for the moment, and at the next moment he may not give it another thought... He is a good companion, jocular, and high-spirited; he does not like to attribute great importance to anything... and he has everybody for a friend... Business tires him, and yet he is restlessly busy with things that are mere play, because this provides change."[63]

Adventurers encourage others to seek "the good life," to join their circle of delight. To live is to play. Every day is a rolling party, requiring companions. Their aptitude for selling the good life to others can extend beyond the personal to commercial and political pursuits. Ever the smiling salesmen, they are skilled at the selling of images, services and products. They have political instincts as well, promoting policies that others may find irresistable.

Concerned with health and appearance, Sevens can become increasingly turned in on themselves. They exude a beauty that may be skin deep only. Owing to their quest for health and beauty, however, they find themselves at war with an opposing tendency to over-indulgence. An ongoing conflict is set in motion between fulfilling appetites and remaining fit. Too many calories, too much night life can take the bloom off the rose.

Sevens are "quick studies," able to rapidly acquire new skills and to immerse themselves in the moment. They have no fear of the new, as long as it promises amusement or challenge. Their grasp of the "real," objective world, and their ability to "use" it skillfully, is singular. Like Fives, they not only "look" but "see." ("It's amazing what you can observe just by watching"—Yogi Berra). Unlike Fives, they tend to put their observations to practical use—often in pursuit of fun. Their sure and steady handling of material reality evokes the *Extraverted Sensation Type* of C. G. Jung: "No other human type can equal [this] type in realism. His sense for objective facts is extraordinarily developed."[64]

Although a quick study, the Seven can become an undisciplined dilettante, displaying a permissiveness towards himself (and others) that causes him to shy from discipline. Despite his remarkable array

---

[63] Immanual Kant, *Anthropology from a Pragmatic Point of View,* p. 198
[64] *Psychological Types,* p. 363

of abilities, he despises restraints and refuses the hard work necessary to turn a natural talent into a developed skill. Why practice if you can "wing it."

Sevens are talented storytellers, witty and detailed. They combine this gift with a wealth of experience, thus enhancing their entertainment value. In doing so, they tend towards redundancy, piling words upon words in the "too-muchness" that characterizes the type. Yet in conversation, as well as action, they steer away from the unpleasant facts of life. The pain of living is pushed out of consciousness by the skills honed during a lifetime of avoidance. For this reason they dislike quiet, preferring to play the stereo, "rev" the engine, chatter, hum, sing and otherwise make noise to counter the threat of emptiness, to ward off a dim awareness that the God who searches minds and hearts is perhaps "closing in."

The Adventurer can develop a rebellious side in opposition to the constraints of a humdrum environment. The attempt to remain free of burdensome duties, as well as the avoidance of unpleasant realities, reflects once again a less-than-serious attitude towards life. It is an attitude that operates against "straight" behavior. It is the attitude of the "wise guy" who shirks his duty, of the guy (or girl) who knows how to "get away with things."

In an unhealthy state, the Seven can slide into a world of make-believe that avoids the real challenges of life. Imagination without application, without the effort to succeed, becomes the norm. Increasingly anxious, the Seven in this state avoids suffering, deprivation and sacrifice at all costs. As he or she spirals into decadence, there is an increasingly frenzied compulsion to fill the inner void with drink, drugs, food or any other means available to quench the pain of suppressed anxiety. Their round of activity becomes increasingly manic. They run faster and faster, like a hamster on a wheel. "They are like the fire of thorns, flashing and crackling for a few minutes, and then quenched for ever."[65] The pleasures for which they grasp become more elusive. Yet they persist in avoidance, attempting to keep at bay their fearful thoughts.

The shallow and sensuous aspects are only one side of the Seven.

---

[65] J. C. Ryle, *Holiness*, p. 75

One can find in this type a disciplined and purposeful individual, too, even as the charm and infectious high spirits remain. Healthy Sevens are refreshing and enthusiastic, friendly, helpful, likely to attract others to share the good times and the good things of life. They learn to appreciate rather than merely consume the gifts and talents they have received. Outgoing and uninhibited, they remain "the life of the party," as well.

David, "the sweet singer of Israel," was a flawed figure who embraced his share of adventure—and folly. A Seven among Sevens, he was—despite his flaws—a man "after God's own heart." He was handsome, passionate, skilled. A man of humble beginnings, he rose "to the top;" a shepherd boy, he became ruler of his people. David, "God's annointed," expressed his vibrant personality as poet, musician, warrior and sovereign. Filled with a lust for life, he danced before the Ark of the Covenant, he composed Psalms, he was zealous in war. He was a man of spontaneity, depth and courage.

Once accustomed to the throne and its prerogatives, David's character weakened. When he saw from his balcony the beautiful Bathsheba, the wife of Uriah the Hittite, he determined to have her, even as Uriah and the king's army were away at war, risking their lives for their king. Yet adultery was only the beginning of David's treachery, of the shameful course of events in which he arranged for the death of Uriah in combat. In sum, "David took Bathsheba (thus, by theft, breaking the eighth commandment) and got her pregnant (thus breaking the seventh) and then to avoid scandal arranged for her husband Uriah to be killed (thus breaking the sixth), and it all began with David coveting his neighbor's wife, in breach of the tenth [commandment]."[66] Not until exposed by the prophet Nathan did the king acknowledge his sins in this sordid episode.

In the years following, David met with success and failure, joy and sorrow. Yet through it all, he remained in his heart of hearts "right" with God. His faith was strong, his devotion enduring. Though his sins were scarlet and his weaknesses many, he was promised an eternal

---

[66] J. I. Packer, *I Want to be a Christian,* p. 304

dynasty. From his line would be traced the Messiah; from his legacy, the idea of a great king.

To transform into a healthier and holier self, Sevens need to "put on the brakes" ("Be still and know that I am God"). Their unceasing activity must be curbed. Besetting sins must be identified and addressed. Renunciation ("oh, no!") is in order: "Renounce the sin that holds you fast—and then you will recover your faith! If you dismiss the word of God's command, you will not receive his word of faith. How can you hope to enter into communion with him when at some point in your life you are running away from him?"[67]

Reflection, too, must be cultivated. "When you are on your beds, search your hearts and be silent" (Psalms 4:4). Folly and overindulgence must be seen for what they are: means to avoid the encounter with the Divine, with finitude, with death. The refusal to control one's activity or to heed wisdom must be counteracted. "How I hated discipline! How my heart spurned correction! I would not obey my teachers or listen to my instructors. I have come to the brink of utter ruin" (Proverbs 5:12-14). All the pleasures in the world leave the compulsed Seven in a sorry state. "All man's efforts are for his mouth, yet his appetite is never satisfied" (Ecclesiastes 7:7).

Far from being a round of novelties and pleasures—the Seven's choice of habitat—the world is often a school of patience and a vale of tears, filled with "losses and crosses." And yet, "Do not make light of the Lord's discipline, and do not lose heart when he rebukes you, because the Lord disciplines those he loves, and he punishes everyone he accepts as a son. Endure hardship as discipline; God is treating you as sons. For what son is not disciplined by his father?" (Hebrews 12: 5-7).

Ouch... but how true and how appropriate. According to the Bible, God is not only tender and merciful but just and severe. He will subject His wayward creatures to the providential circumstances that will mold them into the saved creatures He wants. The process will hurt; it is a slaying of the core self. The Bible, ever the realist, does not veil the hurt of the process. "No discipline seems pleasant at the time, but

---

[67] Dietrich Bonhoeffer, *The Cost of Discipleship,* p. 73

painful. Later on, however, it produces a harvest of righteousness and peace for those who have been trained by it" (Hebrews 12:11). Paul endorses this, agreeing that "we also rejoice in our sufferings, because we know that suffering produces perseverance; perseverance, character; and character, hope" (Romans 5:3-4). Furthermore, he states that "our present sufferings are not worth comparing with the glory that will be revealed in us" (8:18).

Conversion sometimes brings a brief euphoria, a short-lived "upper" to confirm the baby Christian. The joy of "new birth" along with special signs and providences may highlight the entry into new life. In the years that follow, however, challenges and difficulties can be expected. After all, the Christian is called to witness, to worship, to serve. This includes joy, yes, but labor and strife as well. The Seven, and not the Seven alone, needs to be taught about the sterner side of discipleship. Sacrifice, the taking up of one's cross, is a vital part of the journey.

"I do not know how it comes about, but it is nevertheless certain that man gains in stature by voluntary suffering and that general opinion itself thinks the more of him for it... Has any libertine ever discovered a rich courtesan, who sleeps on feathers at midnight, happier than the austere Carmelite, who rises and prays for us at the same hour?"[68] The voluptuary is free to absent himself from grappling with the deep issues of life, the Christian, never.

Sevens need to learn they run a race marked out for them by God. As they face the sometimes unhappy realities of life—face them in faith as they run the providential course—they will find themselves increasingly liberated from their former compulsions. They will learn to live by the Spirit, no longer gratifying "the desires of the sinful nature" (Galatians 5:16). They will find themselves building on rock, not sand, and, firm in faith and conduct, able to face whatever life brings their way.

Adventurers have tried all their lives to taste—and consume—the things which promised pleasure. Redeemed, they look elsewhere for fulfillment. "Taste and see that the LORD is good; blessed is the man who takes refuge in him" (Psalms 34:8).

---

[68] Joseph de Maistre, *The Works of Joseph de Maistre,* p. 261

9

The Leader

"Just as desire and rage multiply our sins, so self-control and humility erase them."
—St. Thalassios the Libyan

"In Hebrew the number eight is... (Sh'moneh), from the root... (Shah'meyn), 'to make fat'... 'to super-abound.' As a participle it means 'one who abounds in strength,' etc. As a noun it is 'superabundant fertility'... as a numeral it is the super-abundant number."[69]

There is nothing particularly "fat" about Type Eight, inasmuch as "fat" indicates "obese" in today's usage (rather than the "richest or choicest part," "firm" or "plenteous" as it does in scripture). There *is* in the Eight, however, a "super-abundance"... in abundance. The Eight is solid, tough-minded, strong, commanding and confrontational, abundantly equipped to face and master the world.

On the wing of the Triad of the Will, Eights are seekers of intensity. Lust is their capital sin; the quest for power, wealth, sex and control, their touchstones. In pursuing their goals they are brave and enterprising. ("Cholerics [the Eight much resembles the choleric type] dream of thunder and of bright, dangerous things."[70]

Immanuel Kant says of the "hot-blooded" choleric that "he is hot-tempered and... is quickly ablaze like a straw fire... His activity is

---
[69] Bullinger, *Number in Scripture,* p. 196
[70] C. S. Lewis, *The Discarded Image,* p. 172

impetuous, but not lasting... He likes to be the chief who makes the decisions, but does not like to carry them out. Consequently, his dominant passion is ambition."[71]

The intelligence of Eights is practical, applied, instinctive, not speculative. Their minds do not spin in circles, they do not second-guess themselves. They pretty much know what they want and "go for it," exercising their strengths to face challenges and overcome obstacles. They embody an "expansive solution: the appeal of mastery."[72]

As noted, Eights strive for wealth, power and control, the very resources they need to reach their chief goal: self-reliance. In their pursuits they can be cunning and sarcastic, pushy and domineering. They neither trust others nor submit to them. The more successful they are in achieving self-reliance—and Eights are often very successful, indeed—the more arrogant and overbearing they may become.

Eights are not detail-oriented, not given to puzzling over particulars. They will sketch out a plan on a napkin over lunch, then leave the management to others. Their contribution to an enterprise is vision, energy and drive.

Eights are always ready to act, to follow a hunch. Aware that one's first hunch is often the right one, they cut to the chase, disregarding irrelevent details and side issues and forging ahead. They make a decision and keep their eye on the ball, even as others become distracted and lose their way. The Eight (in his similarity to the *Extraverted Intuitive*) submits his decisions "to no rational judgment and [relies] entirely on his nose for the possibilities that chance throws in his way."[73]

Eights enjoy competition in all its forms, be it the physical demands of a contact sport or the matching of wits in social or business settings. They like to put pressure on others, to zero in on their vulnerabilities,"to see what they're made of." There is a sheer joy in action, in living intensely, in winning. By contrast, temporarily inactive

---

[71] *Anthropology from a Pragmatic Point of View,* pps. 199-200
[72] Karen Horney
[73] C. G. Jung, *Psychological Types,* p. 368

Eights are unhappy Eights. They "chafe at the bit" without projects. "Because he is always seeking out new possibilities, stable conditions suffocate him."[74]

In the modern era, there is an unbalanced stress on toughness, material achievement and control of the environment, all at the expense of the inner being. It is a world in which the Eight (and not the Eight only) thrives. "In the past most societies tried systematically to discourage somatotonia [W. H. Sheldon's typological formulation most resembling the Eight]. This was a measure of self-defense; they did not want to be physically destroyed by the power-loving aggressiveness of their most active minority, and they did not want to be spiritually blinded by an excess of extraversion."[75] By conrast, our age *is* characterized by "an excess of extraversion."

Eights can be heroes. An example from scripture is Samson, the strong man of Judges. A heroic but flawed figure, a Hercules among Hebrews, his career traces the path of an archaic Eight, with the strengths and weaknesses of that formidable type.

Samson was consecrated a Nazirite ("No razor may be used on his head... [he is] set apart to God from birth."—Judges 13:5), chosen to deliver Israel from the Philistines. Samson lived his life independently, courageously, violently, yet as a protector of the weak and the downtrodden. He was coarse and lustful, visiting a prostitute (chapter 16) and demanding a Philistine woman for his wife ("Get her for me. She's the right one for me."—14:3). He displayed cunning and verbal wit. He was a contriver of riddles.

Samson's superhuman strength accounted for fabulous deeds against the Philistines, whom he slew in their thousands. He killed a young lion as well with his bare hands and burned the fields and vineyards of his enemies by out-foxing the foxes.

The great warrior met his match in the crafty Delilah. Her plotting led to the shearing of Samson's hair, followed by his capture and blinding. Bound in shackles, he was set to grinding in the prison. Yet the hair of the Nazirite grew again. While his enemies mocked him in their temple, God "remembered" him and gave him back his strength.

---

[74] Jung on the *Extraverted Intuitive Type*, Ibid., p. 370
[75] Aldous Huxley, *The Perennial Philosophy,* p. 161

In his final act, he pulled down the temple upon his foes, killing "many more when he died than while he lived" (16:30).

Such was Samson: warrior, hero, chosen vessel. Yet a man, too, of cunning, lust and vengeance, coarse and impetuous. Samson was light and dark, courage and folly. In spite of his vices, he was redeemed. A frightening figure, yes, but a figure some distance above the depths to which the type can sink.

At their lowest depths, Eights become ruthless, merciless and destructive. They may develop a sense of omnipotence and delusions of grandeur. There is a growing obsession with extravagant achievements. They trample upon anyone in their way. In spiraling out of control, they become vengeful and sadistic, ready to intimidate, humiliate or physically injure anyone with the temerity to oppose them.

At the opposite end of the spectrum, the Eight becomes magnanimous. A born crusader, he seeks justice and protects the weak. He aspires after mastery still, but for the good of everyone and not himself alone.

His ability to lead is evident in the bold, steadfast and courageous manner in which he faces challenges, in which he inspires others to follow his example. What he lacks in talent he makes up for in grit. "When the going gets tough, the tough get going." Abounding in stamina, the Eight never gives up and seldom slows down.

Healthy Eights exercise their strength through a surprisingly tender side of their nature. Their tenderness may be connected to the long forgotten "child" who lives within. Perhaps by realizing this "inner child" on some level—this weak and vulnerable self that resides within—Eights are able to reach out to the weak and helpless others who need their succor and protection. Thus the erstwhile tyrant turns out to be—at least from time to time—the embodiment of benevolence.

However, in expressing this kinder, gentler side of themselves, Eights find it difficult to show emotion. "Cuddly bears" they are not. Even so, they expect others to interpret their generous actions as being based in love. Others do not always interpret them so, and the Eight may feel unappreciated.

At their healthiest, Eights can become big-hearted, merciful, ready to take the weak and downtrodden under their wing. In this—to their credit—they seek justice ("For the LORD is righteous, he loves justice; upright men will see his face." Psalms 11:7). Their sense of fairness comes to the fore, to the benefit of the needy and the oppressed. Also, they learn to forgive injury and insult, no longer harboring petty resentments. They are, after all, tough; they can take it.

Eights like to prove their mettle in the physical realm, to "build big" in ways that are tangible, to demonstrate their strength for all to see. As means to their own independence and security, as pathways to inflating their own egos, such activity may indeed bear fruit. As the life goal of a Christian, it "misses the mark" (the very definition of *hamartia,* sin). Yet scoring points in the physical world (attaining high political office, becoming a tycoon, commanding a military campaign—the very things a high-flying Eight might do) is not, in itself, either good or bad for the soul's health. It depends on one's relationship—on one's essentially secret and interior relationship—to the Divine.

Where one's heart is, one's treasure is. When Eights put their "heart and soul" into their worldly enterprises, when they are consumed by them without remainder, they have departed from the Way, the Truth and the Life, settling instead for that which moth and rust do corrupt. Thus worldly achievement brings to the Eight no real peace. "What does a man get for all the toil and anxious striving with which he labors under the sun?... Even at night his mind does not rest" (Ecclesiastes 2:22-23). Before long, Eights—so recently pleased with their latest triumph—are dreaming of new schemes and conquests.

Eights, so adroit at using the things of this world, need to learn that wealth and power are properly means, not ends. The human essence, made in the image of God, partakes of immortality. It will outlast the works of the flesh, the transient achievements of the passing world. Thus it is vital to enter into the relationship that lasts. Paradoxically, such a relationship may even bring an increase in earthly blessings: "Honor the LORD with your wealth, with the first fruits of all your crops; then your barns will be filled to overflowing, and your vats will brim over with new wine" (Proverbs 3:9-10).

The powerful Christian is called to protect the weak and to seek justice, to be a tribune of the downtrodden. He is to lead a life of self-control, channeling his aggressive instincts into good works and away from temptations to violence. "Refrain from anger and turn from wrath; do not fret—it leads only to evil. For evil men will be cut off, but those who hope in the LORD will inherit the land" (Psalms 37:8-9). Hope in the Lord is given priority, not the emotions of anger and wrath, no matter how justified they might seem. Instead, believers are counseled to "Make every effort to live in peace with all men and to be holy; without holiness no one will see the Lord" (Hebrews 12:14).

Eights, when they begin to feel their tempers flare, should take a deep breath and "count to ten." They need perspective on themselves and the situations they find themselves in. They need to know that a non-violent response to provocation can pack a greater punch than a violent response. A peaceful word to an adversary may very well "heap burning coals on his head" (Romans 12:20); in other words, impart a burning sense of shame. A mild reply can work a sort of "spiritual jujitsu," "throwing" an opponent by the weight of his own evil intent. Such is God's preferred method: to short-circuit violence by breaking its patterns of escalating conflict. "A patient man has great understanding, but a quick-tempered man displays folly" (Proverbs 14:29).

In the teaching of Christ, the command to treat others in loving ways ("So in everything, do to others what you would have them do to you, for this sums up the law and the prophets."—Matthew 7:12) goes to the greatest of lengths: "But I tell you: Love your enemies and pray for those who persecute you, that you may be sons of your Father in heaven. He causes his sun to rise on the evil and the good, and sends rain on the righteous and the unrighteous... Be perfect, therefore, as your heavenly Father is perfect" (5:44-45).

Thus the Christian is to treat others with justice and mercy—be they evil or good, righteous or unrighteous—even as the Father does. The world teaches "an eye for an eye;" the powerful Eight *exacts* an eye for an eye (and sometimes an arm or a leg for an eye). This inverts the Christian rule. Enemies should be treated in a Godly manner, perfectly. ("Perfect" in this sense does not mean without fault but rather, as the Greek literally says, "brought to completion." It is out of this "completion," or state of fulfillment and wholeness, that the Eight can find the strength and inner peace to extend peace to others, even enemies).

One can find similarly irenic teaching in St. Paul, where the Apostle urges the following: "Don't have anything to do with foolish and stupid arguments, because you know they produce quarrels. And the Lord's servant must not quarrel; instead, he must be kind to everyone. Those who oppose him he must gently instruct in the hope that God will grant them repentance leading them to a knowledge of the truth" (2 Timothy 2:23-25). "Gently instruct" is the key. The Eight is inclined to be far from gentle.

Alexander Whyte, in recommending a prayer to cholerics, limns (in fine Victorian flourish) the desiderata of an integrating Eight: "Lord, let me be ever courteous and easy to be intreated. Never let me fall into a peevish or contentious spirit. Let me follow peace with all men, offering forgiveness, inviting them by courtesies, ready to confess my own errors, apt to make amends, and desirous to be reconciled. Give me the spirit of a Christian, charitable, humble, merciful and meek, useful and liberal, angry at nothing but my own sins, and grieving for the sins of others, that, while my passion obeys my reason, and my reason is religious, and my religion is pure and undefiled, managed with humility, and adorned with charity, I may escape thy anger, which I have deserved, and may dwell in thy love, and be thy son and servant forever."[76]

Ultimately, the Eight—the healthy and integrating Eight—realizes that God provides the only firm foundation. Next to this, the material foundation of self-reliance crumbles, the power-ego is humbled. "Humble yourselves, therefore, under his mighty hand, and he will raise you up in due time" (1 Peter 5:6). Yes, *God* will "raise up." God will use the strength of the Leader in His time, at His choosing. The Eight at rest in this will know the peace that passes all understanding.

---

[76] Tim LaHaye, *Transformed Temperaments,* p. 149, quoting from *Treasury of Alexander Whyte*

10

The Peacemaker

"I have so much to do that I am going to bed."
—Savoyard proverb

Nine "is the *last* of the digits, and thus marks the *end;* and is significant of the *conclusion* of a matter... it is thus significant of the *end of man,* and the summation of all man's works.... It marks the completeness, the end and issue of all things as to man—the judgment of man and all his works."[77]

The Type Nine personality *is* a "conclusion" and a "summation" of all things human; indeed, the prototype of the types, according to at least one Enneagram authority. Richard Rohr, in his *Discovering the Enneagram: An Ancient Tool for a New Spiritual Journey,* co-authored with Andreas Ebert, says "It's no accident that the NINES are situated at the vertex of the Enneagram, because in a certain way NINE describes the original and unspoiled human essence. We would probably all be NINES, if we hadn't grown up in a technologically 'civilized' world."[78]

The Nine, however, is a prototype under judgment, as is everything regarding "man and all his works." The Nine, like other types, is marked by sin. There is in humankind no "unspoiled essence" this side of the Fall.

---

[77] E. W. Bullinger, *Number in Scripture,* p. 235
[78] p. 162

Located in the center of the Will Triad, the Nine is a "gut" type along with the Eight and the One. It is akin to C. G. Jung's *Introverted Sensation* type, it exemplifies one of Horney's "self-effacing solutions."

Strong-willed like its adjacent types, the Nine expresses in his or her personality the capital sin of "sloth." Phlegmatic and often withdrawn, the Nine is willful in maintaining stasis, like a motorist pressing on the brake and the accelerator at the same time. In the unflattering words of Thomas Elyot, the phlegmatic type—of which the Nine is an example—is characterized by "fatnesse... colour white... sleepe superfluous (i..e. in excess)... dremes of things watery or of fish... slownesse... dulnesses of lerning... smallness of courage."[79]

By contrast, Kant evokes a more balanced assessment of the type, whom he says is "not stirred easily or quickly, but, if slowly, then persistently. He who has a good dose of phlegm in him warms up slowly; but he holds the warmth longer. He does not get angry easily... His fortunate temperament takes the place of wisdom, and even in ordinary life people often call him the philosopher. By virtue of this temperament he is superior to others without offending their vanity. Frequently he is cunning, because all the bullets and missiles fired at him bounce off him as from a sack of wool."[80]

Nines long to be in union—in balance and harmony—with people, nature, God and the cosmos. But in seeking balance and harmony in their lowest common denominator, they can be passive, resigned, neglectful, undeveloped and obstinate.

Nines are life's late starters, characterized by a lack of motivation and an absence of goals ("Such a type can easily make one question why one should exist at all"[81]). They think, in contemplating action, "that others can do it better" than they. When they do seek and aspire, it is generally in an unfocused manner with poor concentration. They are conflicted, with aspects of self split asunder in spite of their longing for unity. The inner conflict, and the manner in which it is dampened and depressed, renders their condition static.

---

[79] C. S. Lewis, *The Discarded Image,* p. 173

[80] *Anthropology from a Pragmatic Point of View,* pp. 200-201

[81] Jung, on the *Introverted Sensation Type* in *Psychological Types,* p. 395

Sloth, which today indicates mental or physical laziness (and puts one in mind of the slow-moving arboreal creature of that name), was called "accidie" in the Middle Ages. In that period it had a more comprehensive and deeper meaning. It involved a refusal of God's grace, of His offer of help, opportunity and growth. "Accidie is partial consent to non-being, striking a bargain with insignificance."[82]

Sloth, as understood today, is but a part of accidie. The Nine, as a type, incorporates both the traditional and the current meaning. In the words of Alexander Whyte:

> Sloth [and here, in addressing the phlegmatic personality, he could be describing an average Nine] sums up, in one short and expressive word, the bad side of this temperament. Some part of what we call sloth in men is, no doubt, in fairness to be set down to such a phlegmatic constitution that it would take the will and the energy of a giant to overcome it. There are men of such a slow-working heart, their blood creeps through their veins at such a snail's pace, their joints are so loosely knit, and their whole body is so lethargic, that both God and man must take all into consideration before they condemn them. And when we say sloth in this case, we still take into account all that can be said in extenuation, and the phlegmatic man will not be blamed for what he could not help. He will be blamed and chastised only for what he could well have helped if only he had resolved to help it. At the same time, sloth is sloth, laziness is laziness, whatever your temperament may be. Laziness, indeed, is not of the body at all; it is of the mind.[83]

To reinforce inner peace, the Nine maintains regular habits. There is a clinging to "security blankets," a special enjoyment of games, hobbies, forms of passive entertainment (watching television, listening to music). Nines collect knicknacks or tinker with gadgets. They enjoy

---

[82] William S. Stafford, *Disordered Loves, Healing the Seven Deadly Sins,* p. 113

[83] Tim LaHaye, *Transformed Temperaments,* pp. 197-198, quoting from *Treasury of Alexander Whyte*

"homey" surroundings, where they dwell among the familiar and the cozy. They are content to identify with a group—a family, club, sports team or nation—to obtain a sense of self. This compensates, at least in part, for their belittling of themselves. Seemingly safe in their routines and protected environments, they find themselves "oriented amid the flux of events not by rational judgment but simply by what happens."[84]

Nines tend to be socially stable, with an unreflective and underdeveloped interior life. They avoid the effort of hard, critical thought, accepting instead the commonplaces of their milieau. They are undisturbed by self-examination. Yet "men are without excuse" (Romans 1:20). There is spiritual obligation among the "once-born," inner work required. They need to ask, seek and knock, to search out the Divine both within and without. But the Nine, like the *Introverted Sensation* type, "is uncommonly inaccessible to objective understanding, and... usually fares no better in understanding himself."[85]

The Nine can be stubborn and passive-resistant (or passive-aggressive), whether or not the demands of others are appropriate. Thus, Nines are difficult to exploit. They balk at decisions and deadlines. They resist if they think they are being asked to do too much. When they do accede to a request, they do what is asked and no more. It is not for them to go above and beyond the call of duty. By such means, they protect their freedom.

Imperturbable and sluggish, Nines are more than content "to wait on the Lord." They heed not the Word, with its droll example of diligence: "Go to the ant, you sluggard. Consider its ways and be wise!... How long will you lie there, you sluggard? When will you get up from your sleep?" (Proverbs 6:6-9). Unlike the ant, Nines are little moved by inner resolve. They rely, rather, on external stimuli to nudge them into action.

Despite their sluggish tendencies, Nines do use plenty of energy. In doing so they exercise their will, albeit in a largely instinctive and unconscious manner. Most of this energy is devoted to remaining

---

[84] Jung, on the *Introverted Sensation Type* in *Psychological Types,* p. 395
[85] Ibid., p. 397

immobile. As noted above, they push on the brake and the accelerator simultaneously. Or, to change metaphors, they "run fast" to maintain stasis, causing wear and tear on body and soul and leaving the themselves subject to fatigue and depression.

Owing to their equilibrium of sloth, Nines often speak in a monotone and show little expression or animation in the face. They often listen and respond to others inattentively. They say "yes" but do not really mean it. Rather, the "yes" is a short-sighted means to avoid conflict. This can lead to misunderstandings and strained relationships. ("The type becomes a menace to his environment because his total innocuousness is not altogether above suspicion."[86])

Unhealthy Nines increasingly refuse to recognize painful facts. By this means, they escape intimations of failure and lack of self development. They escape as well, for a time, the anxieties such thoughts are bound to produce. They remain out of touch with the springs of action that motivate others and could be used to motivate themselves, inhabiting instead their personal Walden Pond of peace and simplicity.

Disintegrating Nines can become angry and defiant, reacting against those who try to coax them into a more directed and energetic mode of living. Yet try as they might to avoid acknowledging their increasingly unhappy circumstances, Nines may reach the moment of truth in which they can no longer repress their failures and self-defeating strategies. The earlier, easygoing self may become anxious, agitated, overly emotional, even abusing drink or drugs.

Nines, of course, have their virtues, with generosity and liberality among them. They are also able to endure trying situations with patience, to sustain others in trouble and to serve as a foundation of support for those close to them. They are generally good-natured and calm. They are steady under pressure.

As they integrate to a healthier self, Nines learn to become more assertive. They become "doers of the word, not hearers only." Gone is the "shrinking violet." The Nine becomes "a presence in the room," ready to play a constructive role in the life of society.

---

[86] Ibid., p. 397

Also, owing to their dispassionate tempers, they are able (when they make the attempt) to be attentive listeners, a skill useful in helping others solve their problems. They make excellent mediators. "Blessed are the peacemakers, for they will be called sons of God" (Matthew 5:9). Harmony, balance, equilibrium—the type's most longed-for qualities—are thus realized in themselves and others.

The Patriarch Abraham bears the marks of the Nine. Raised amidst the idolatry of Ur of the Chaldees, "Abram" showed himself passive and obedient before the revelatory God of scripture. In response to a marvelous theophany, he left his native land and sought a promised destiny. A city-dweller, he became a nomad, drifting with his flocks and herds, assured by the Divine Word of countless descendents and a homeland for his people.

This phlegmatic progenitor of the Hebrews demonstrated time and again his inclination to pursue peace and harmony, whether for good or ill. When conflict developed between his herdsmen and the herdsmen of his nephew, Lot, Abraham allowed Lot to choose the better part of the land. "Let's not have any quarreling between you and me" (Genesis 13:8). So, too, when the Lord made clear his determination to destroy Sodom, Abraham pleaded on behalf of the city's righteous inhabitants, evincing his pacific, merciful tendencies. When, on two occasions, he feared for his life at the hands of foreigners, he showed his passivity—indeed, his fear and timidity— by attempting to pass off his wife, Sarah (Sarai), as his sister, an act of expediency and cowardice. (On the other hand, Abraham could, in his stolid nature, show a cool head and stubborn determination. He demonstrated courage and tactical skill when he led his armed men in the attack that rescued Lot from the four kings).

Abraham showed himself as pliable in the hands of Sarah as in the hands of God. At the instigation of his wife, he had intercourse with Sarah's maid, Hagar, to assure an heir. When she became pregnant, Hagar "began to despise her mistress" (Genesis 16:4). Stung, an irate Sarah blamed *Abraham* for the unhappy situation. In typically meek fashion, Abraham bore his wife's anger and gave Sarah permission to do what she wished. As a result, the maid was expelled for a time. (Of her illegitimate union with Abraham, Ishmael was born).

In the course of time, God fulfilled his promise to Abraham and Sarah by giving them a son of their own, Isaac. At the time Isaac was weaned, Sarah observed Ishmael mocking her son. She again ordered Abraham (with "backup" from God) to expel Ishmael and Hagar from their midst. Abraham—conflicted, passive but ever obedient—did so.

Not surprisingly, Isaac was the apple of Abraham's eye. Yet when God demanded the sacrifice of Isaac—in one of Scripture's most harrowing passages—Abraham showed himself characteristically pliant, though undoubtedly anguished. He expressed his faith, his trust, in God to the greatest extent. In the end, divine intervention prevented the boy's sacrifice, even as Abraham was utterly vindicated in God's sight. "Now I know that you fear God" (Genesis 22:12).

The healthy Nine is one thing, the unhealthy, another. Even the Nine who is a Christian—a serious Christian—is not free from danger. Sloth and passivity can trap the unwary. "It is possible for a consecrated Christian to be deceived into passivity for some years without ever awakening to his dangerous plight. The degree of inactivity will increase in scope until he suffers unspeakable pain in mind, emotion, body and environment. To present the true meaning of consecration to these ones thus becomes vitally important. The knowledge of truth is absolutely necessary for deliverance from passivity, without which freedom is *impossible.* We know that a believer falls into passivity through deception but this latter in turn is caused by a lack of knowledge. The very first step to freedom is to know the truth of all things: truth concerning cooperation with God, the operation of evil spirits, consecration, and supernatural manifestations."[87] To know "the truth of all things"—the truth of all things pertinent to the spiritual malady at issue—is indeed a *big* "first step" but a necessary one.

Obedience to the precepts of God is life-changing. "The law of the Lord is perfect, reviving the soul. The statutes of the Lord are trustworthy, making wise the simple" (Psalms 19:7). Elsewhere the Psalmist says: "I have more understanding than the elders, for I obey

---

[87] Watchman Nee, *The Spiritual Man,* Vol. 3, p. 120

your precepts" (119:99). And then this: "Though I am lowly and despised, I do not forget your precepts" (Psalms 119:141). Even the most self-deprecating of Nines can take heart from these words. Obedience to God, and the integrity and strength that emanate from it, stirs the phlegmatic soul to action. "Never be lacking in zeal, but keep your spiritual fervor, serving the Lord" (Romans 12:11).

According to the Apostle Paul (in 1 Corinthians), everyone in the church is a vital member of the Body of Christ. The key to service is availability. Nines need to "be present" in spirit, soul and body, to take their rightful place, to let their light shine and their good deeds be manifest. They should be open to opportunities; they should pray upon them before turning them down. They should recall that "Whoever sows sparingly will also reap sparingly, and whoever sows generously will also reap generously" (2 Corinthians 9:6).

Nines need to persist, to be hopeful, to be watchful, to be in the thick of life. For "Unlike orchids [Christians] do not grow as hothouse plants. Jesus did not live the life of a hothouse plant, evading life's abrasiveness, and he does not intend that his disciples should either."[88] Nines need to unearth their buried talent and put it to use in ways that glorify God, serve others, and fulfill themselves.

In meditating on the Lord's Prayer, C. S. Lewis discovered a surprise meaning in the petition, "Thy will *be done.*" In putting the emphasis on the last two words, he came to realize that much of what needed to be done was to be done by God's servants, himself included. "The petition, then, is not merely that I may patiently suffer God's will but also that I may vigorously do it. I must be an agent as well as a patient. I am asking [in prayer] that I may be enabled to do it."[89]

The Nine must face the difficulties, challenges and troubles of life, both exterior and interior, in carrying out the will of God. This is not easy for anyone, especially for one inclined to sloth. For there is nothing "we naturally dislike so much as 'trouble' about our religion. We hate trouble. We secretly wish we could have a vicarious Christianity, and could be good by proxy, and have everything done for us. Anything that requires exertion and labour is entirely against

[88] J. I. Packer, *Rediscovering Holiness,* p. 188
[89] *Letters to Malcolm, Chiefly on Prayer,* pps. 25-26

the grain of our hearts. But the soul can have 'no gains without pains'... To be a Christian it will cost a man his love of ease."[90]

The Nine, like everyone else, is called to service, to step into his or her role on the stage of life and become something other than a passive observer. Jesus Christ wants His servants to be alive with a zest for life. The Nine is thereby warned that transformation is needed. One must begin to walk in the paths prepared for him "before the foundation of the world," the paths that are ever new, ever old, and ever open to the obedient servant.

---

[90] Bishop J. C. Ryle, *Holiness,* p. 69

11

The Striver

*"I have done nothing good before Thee, but grant me, in
Thy compassion, the power to make a start."*
—Arsenios of Egypt

"There can be no doubt as to the significance of the primary number. It is the symbol of unity... 'One' excludes all difference, for there is no second with which it can either harmonize or conflict."[91]

Type One, "The Striver," seeks indeed to exclude "all difference," esteeming itself as the repository of the ONE RIGHT WAY of doing things. Ones do not easily "harmonize" (but most certainly "conflict") with others or themselves.

Melancholic and choleric by turn, they are found in the Triad of the Will. Owing to anger, their root sin, they are critical by nature. They are, when less than healthy, akin to Jung's *Extraverted Thinking Type,* a figure who combines the principled rationalist and the carping critic, who is a "sultry and resentful character... Magnanimous as he may be in sacrificing himself to his intellectual goal, his feelings are petty, mistrustful, crotchety, and conservative."[92]

Even as Ones are afraid of being condemned, they are quick to condemn others. They project a sense of vileness onto their neighbor, then berate themselves with equal fervor. ("I do not know what the heart of a rascal may be; I know what is in the heart of an honest man;

---

[91] Bullinger, *Number in Scripture,* p. 50
[92] *Psychological Types,* p. 350

it is horrible."—Joseph de Maistre). Their stance is dualistic: their self-loathing is the inverse of their self-righteousness.

"In your anger do not sin" (Ephesians 4:26). Good counsel, yet Ones find it difficult to keep indignation and resentment fully suppressed. At war with themselves, Ones are at war with others and anger "will out," if not in a tantrum then in facial tics, compulsive gestures, rigidity. They "stew in their own juices."

Kant, for his part, writes that the "heavy-blooded" melancholy (in which aspects of the One can be seen) "directs his attention first of all to difficulties, while the sanguine person relies on the hope of success. Therefore the melancholy person thinks deeply, just as the sanguine thinks only superficially... [The melancholy is] uneasy, mistrusting, and critical, thereby also incapacitating him for joyfulness."[93]

Ones are impatient with themselves and others. Instead of accepting the necessity of process, of step-by-step advance, they strive hurriedly for completion. Beginnings, by nature partial and imperfect, conflict with their psychic ideal. They find it hard to begin a task, hard to get the "flow" of activity going. They aspire to get it right *right* now, today, not tomorrow. In fact, Ones generally *do* get things right, to the annoyance of the less particular. "Lesser mortals" need to follow suit. There are standards to be upheld, everyone should adhere to them, everyone should "get it right."

Not everyone "gets it right," not to the One's satisfaction. Thus Ones tend to monopolize tasks and responsibilities, marginalizing others and tending towards "workaholism." They resist delegating. "If you want something done right, do it yourself." But this is short-sighted, unsatisfactory to themselves and others. It heightens their awareness of how much they have to do and of how little time they have to do it in. Thus their sense of time is "pressurized." Ones, if they would integrate to a healthier self, need to summon the help of others, to cooperate with those others and be enriched by them. D. L Moody used to say, "Instead of doing the work of ten men, get ten men to work." This is shrewd advice. A similar policy was suggested by Jethro, the priest of Midian, when he advised Moses to select judges

---

[93] *Anthropology from a Pragmatic Point of View,* p. 199

to ease the burden of governing. Moses, wisely, accepted the advice of his father-in-law, to his and the people's gain.

The critical inner voice which inhabits the psyche of Ones curbs spontaneity and causes them to interrupt themselves, to correct their own speech and to argue against themselves. This criticality reinforces the tendency to be judgmental and reductionist, and makes them akin to the *Extraverted Thinking Type* who "elevates objective reality, or an objectively oriented intellectual formula, into the ruling principle not only for himself but for his whole environment. By this formula good and evil are measured, and beauty and ugliness determined. Everything that agrees with this formula is right, everything that contradicts it is wrong, and anything that passes by it indifferently is merely incidental."[94]

Heightened criticality, however, has an upside. Like the double-edged sword of God's word, the One "penetrates even to dividing soul and spirit, joints and marrow" (Hebrews 4:12), drawing the sharpest distinctions, discerning right and wrong, just and unjust. Ones are lucid thinkers and rigorous reasoners (deductive in method), compelled to be honest. They see through the pretenses of the phony, they ferret out the deceiver.

In a related vein, Ones incline to scrupulosity, they "strain out gnats and swallow camels." They are sticklers for detail. Everything should be in its place and there should be a place for everything. They apply their scrupulosity to mundane matters as well as to higher levels of concern, to moral behavior, spiritual practice and philosophy. These disciplines, to please a One, must be consistent and true in all their parts; in short, they must be perfect. Yet "excessive scruple is only hidden pride."—Goethe.

Ones are incensed if things are not fair. They are seekers of justice, not only for themselves but for others, or in the name of an abstract ideal. They want things to be as they *should* be. The One is steadfast for truth, even when it hurts. Extroverted thinkers, they are on a mission to reform, to "teach and preach," to witness to the truth as they see it.

Ones find it hard to let go of their striving because they believe

---

[94] Jung, *Psychological Types*, p. 347

they must be perfect to be loved and accepted. The selfless love of God for his wayward creatures, His reaching out to imperfect beings while they are yet sinners, are data of faith that seem to elude them. Yet, in the divine economy, the faithful are totally sinners and totally just. By grace they are saved, through faith, not works, so that no one can boast.

Martin Luther (who suffered greatly from scruples) says in his *Commentary on Galatians* that his superior, Staupitz, was inclined to say, "I have vowed unto God above a thousand times that I would become a better man: but I never performed that which I vowed. Hereafter I will make no such vow: for I have now learned by experience that I am not able to perform it. Unless, therefore, God be favorable."[95] Staupitz, a good but flawed man, expressed the wisdom of maturity, fully aware that grace alone would see him through.

The Apostle Paul—enthusiastic, charismatic, even mystical—bears the marks of a One. Introduced in the Book of Acts as one "breathing and threatening slaughter" towards the new sect of the Christians, this zealous Pharisee was all his life bent on righting the wrongs of the world. Following his dramatic conversion to the Christian faith, he continued his crusading ways, a personality with a purpose, a choleric-melancholic bundle of focused energy.

As a One, Paul was logical: "For if the dead are not raised, then Christ has not been raised either. And if Christ has not been raised, your faith is futile" (1 Corinthians 15:16-17).

He was disciplined: "I beat my body and make it my slave" (1 Corinthians 9:27).

He had a keen conscience: "So I strive always to keep my conscience clear before God and man" (Acts 24:16).

He put principles and purpose ahead of comfort: "I have learned the secret of being content in any and every situation, whether well fed or hungry, whether living in plenty or in want" (Philippians 4:12-13).

He knew his imperfections: "Christ Jesus came into the world to save sinners—of whom I am the worst" (1 Timothy 1:15).

---

[95] William James, *The Varieties of Religious Experience,* p. 129

He liked to preach and teach: "So Paul stayed for a year and a half, teaching them the word of God" (Acts 18:11).

He came down hard on antinomians and slackers: "Shall we go on sinning so that grace may increase? By no means!" (Romans 6:1-2).

He was eager to vindicate himself before the bar of justice: "'I am now standing before Caesar's court, where I ought to be tried... I appeal to Caesar'" (Acts 25:10-11).

He was not above getting in the last word: "Men, you should have taken my advice not to sail from Crete; then you would have spared yourselves this damage and loss" (Acts 27:21).

Throughout his singular life, Paul remained a morally serious person, mystically identified with his Savior, humbled by a "thorn in the flesh," and enraptured by the grace of God—and not his own works—in which he found all meaning and purpose.

Ones need to "loosen up," to enjoy life. This is—for a One—harder than it seems. Even in pursuit of leisure, the One is likely to try too hard, to attempt to force the issue. "Are we having fun yet?" There is, in this regard, a crying need to address oneself, to "back-talk" the super ego and its insistence that every moment be filled with vital matters. The Bible (yes, that somber tome bound in black leather) can be of help. Ecclesiastes, for example, endorses the deep but simple joys of everyday living:

- "So I commend the enjoyment of life, because nothing is better for a man under the sun than to eat and drink and be glad" (8:15).

- "A man can do nothing better than to eat and drink, and find satisfaction in his work. This... is from the hand of God, for without him, who can eat or find enjoyment" (2:24-25).

- "Light is sweet, and it pleases the eyes to see the sun. However many years a man may live, let him enjoy them all" (11:7-8).

Ones need to be thankful for what is, not obsessed with what might be. "Be joyful always; pray continually; give thanks in all circumstances, for this is God's will for you in Christ Jesus" (1 Thessalonians 5:16-18).

Ones need to curb their unhealthy attachment to life's rules and regulations. A sense of proportion is needed. Principles and rules, though good and helpful in themselves, can blind a person to weightier matters. This does not imply that a One should abdicate concern for right and wrong. It cautions, rather, that by themselves, no amount of striving, no amount of outward obedience, will advance one's sanctification. No human performance "is ever good enough. There are always wrong desires in the heart, along with a lack of right ones, regardless of how correct one's outward motions are.. and it is at the heart that God looks first."[96] Effort, if undertaken in mindfulness of one's relationship to God, *is* commendable and profitable. Lacking that relationship, it is ultimately futile.

Another item of concern is "the voice in the back of one's head." Conscience, that highly charged faculty within the psyche of the One must be consulted with care, as it may be misinformed or conditioned to place arbitrary rules before love. In addition, it may be dulled by repeated sins. In such cases, conscience does not speak the wisdom of God. Further, the consciences of many are formed almost completely by family and community standards and are thus of limited use. The conscience must be imprinted with the wisdom of scripture to be useful and reliable. The One, who tends to identify conscience with the voice of God, needs especially to heed this caution.

Still another area of concern is the inclination to be judgmental, to hold grudges, to brood on real or fancied slights. Ones mistakenly think an offending party should know that he or she is in the wrong, that confrontation is thus unnecessary and unseemly. The cold shoulder, the slow burn, the unspoken grievance take the place of confrontation and resolution. In this, Ones are clearly wrong. Better it is to face the object of their anger and "clear the air" as suggested by William Blake:

---

[96] J. I. Packer, *Concise Theology*, p. 173

I was angry with my friend:
I told my wrath, my wrath did end.
I was angry with my foe:
I told it not, my wrath did grow.

In maturing, Ones need to work at becoming "process" persons. They cannot by force of will order into being the circumstances they might wish. God determines the seasons; He has His own timetable. He will open and close doors, block and unblock paths, make smooth the road along which He wishes His subjects to travel. "No man can order his life... The one secret of life and development is not to devise and plan to but to fall in with the forces at work—to do every moment's duty aright—that being the part in the process alotted to us: and let come—not what will, for there is no such thing—but what the eternal thought wills for each of us, has intended in each of us from the first."[97]

Striving in one's own strength provides neither peace nor sanctity. Faith is required first and faith is a gift, not a product of striving. "Faith may result in action, and certainly true faith in Jesus always will result in action; but faith itself is not doing but receiving."[98] Imbued with authentic faith, one is enabled to act within the proper context of being. There is no longer any illusion of a self-made state of perfection. Jesus alone, apart from the striving of the One, "is the author and perfecter of our faith" (Hebrews 12:2).

---

[97] C. S. Lewis, quoting George MacDonald in *George MacDonald, An Anthology,* pps. 154-155
[98] J. Gresham Machen, *What is Faith,* p. 89

12

A Word About Wings

"There is as much difference between us and ourselves as between us and others."
—Michel de Montaigne

"Wings" are the types on either side of a person's basic type. For instance, if a person is a Five, he or she will have either a Four or a Six wing. The wing will color that person's "Fiveness." Thus a Five with a Four wing will manifest certain characteristics of the Four (some tendency to emotionalism or artistic temperament, perhaps) while a Five with a Six wing will manifest certain characteristics of the Six (a sense of team spirit or insecurity).

The concept of wings is an important one as it sheds light on the types and their complexities. It should be noted that the subject has been discussed at length elsewhere, most thoroughly in *Personality Types, Using the Enneagram for Self Discovery,* by Don Richard Riso and Russ Hudson.

Although there is no need to discuss the theory of wings in any detail here, readers unfamiliar with the Enneagram might wish to have some idea of how the concept is used. Thus the types and their wings, in brief compass, appear as follows:

The Two with a One wing experiences conflict between the "emotional, interpersonal and histrionic" traits of the Two[99] and the

---

[99] Riso-Hudson, p. 90

rational, impersonal and self-controlled traits of the One. The subtype has a strong conscience (compliments of the One) that militates against the urge to act always according to emotional needs. There are conflicts between "head" and "heart." By contrast, the traits of the Two and those of the Three-wing tend to reinforce each other, as both types relate easily to people.

The Three with a Two wing has highly developed interpersonal skills, as the traits of the Three and the Two wing complement each other. The subtype tends to be the "center of attention" and "extremely charming."[100] By contrast, the traits of the Three and the Four wing are often in conflict. The interpersonal Three is influenced by the withdrawing Four, resulting in a subtype that looks quite different— and more private—than the stereotypically outgoing and social Three.

The Four with a Three wing exhibits a measure of inner conflict, as the principal type works to harmonize the search for inner authenticity with the Three's easy ability to project an image popular with others. By contrast, the traits of Fours and Fives are congenial, with the Five adding intellectual depth.

The Five with a Four wing faces considerable conflict, as the cerebral, stand-offish Five cannot always deal comfortably with the emotionalism of the Four. The subtype is a "rich" one, however, "combining possibilities for oustanding artistic as well as intellectual achievement."[101] By contrast, the traits of the Five and a Six wing complement each other but not always in happy ways. The distrustfulness of both types diminishes the effectiveness of their interpersonal relations.

The Six with a Five wing evinces a conflict of traits, as the principal type is characterized by dependency on others while the Five is detached. By contrast, the traits of the Six harmonize with those of a Seven wing. In this instance, there is a tendency for the dutiful Six to be more extroverted and sociable.

The Seven with a Six wing experiences a measure of disharmony, inasmuch as the Six is "oriented toward people" while "Sevens are oriented towards things and experiences."[102] Sevens take care of their

---

[100] Ibid., p. 128
[101] Ibid., p. 210
[102] Ibid, p. 291

own needs. The Seven with an Eight wing, a "real presence in the room," is a personality of which others take note. The traits of both are aggressive, and the subtype is doubly aggressive.

The Eight with a Seven wing is, again—owing to the resonance of the two types—a very aggressive subtype. In fact, owing to the dominance of the Eight, this is the *most* aggressive and most egocentric of the subtypes. By contrast, there is some conflict between the traits of an Eight and those of a Nine wing. Here, the wing curbs the aggressive stance and makes the subtype more interested in other people.

The Nine with an Eight wing exhibits a measure of conflict, as the traits of the Nine tend towards passivity and good relations with others, while the Eight wing adds a degree of strong self-assertion. By contrast, the traits of the Nine and those of a One wing are mostly harmonious. Here both types repress their emotions but for different reasons, the Nine to maintain peace and the One to maintain self-control.

The One with a Nine wing enjoys a harmony of traits, as each component of the subtype distances itself from the environment, creating a somewhat cool and detached personality. There is, on the other hand, a measure of conflict in a One with a Two wing. The controlled, rational One becomes warmer and more involved with others, more of a "people person."

An additional refinement of the Enneagram system, the "levels of development," is an original teaching of Riso's that uses a nine-level continuum within each type to better understand the movements from healthy to average to unhealthy states and then back again.

Yet another refinement is the theory of instinctual subtypes, these being the self-preservation, social and sexual instincts. These, too (first taught by Oscar Ichazo), have been elaborated elsewhere, as in the Riso-Hudson book already mentioned, wherein they are called "instinctual variants."

13

Spirit and Soul

"The Chest—Magnanimity—Sentiment—these are the indispensable liaison officers between cerebral man and visceral man. It may even be said that it is by this middle element that man is man: for by his intellect he is mere spirit and by his appetite mere animal."
—C. S. Lewis, *The Abolition of Man*

In the modern view, man is diminished. He is marginalized, secularized, relativized. He is lonely, the orphan of the universe. In the past, he was a creature of dignity and importance, wounded in his nature but theomorphic in essence. He had fallen but he was redeemable. God was mindful of him.

Also, in traditional understanding, man was tripartite, consisting of spirit, soul and body. Christian doctrine reflected this in the Latin *spiritus, anima* and *corpus*. In Greek, the triad was *pneuma, psyche* and *soma*. (Islam, too, contrasted spirit and soul with *ruh* and *nafs*, as did Hebrew, with *ruach* and *nephesh*).

As the Western understanding passed by degrees from the traditional to the modern view, spirit and soul were confused and conflated. The person became dichotomous and thus, diminished. The *single* entity "spirit-soul" became a ghost in the machine and, in time, all but vanished.

This "machine" of modernity (and "post-modernity" as well) does, to be sure, have within it an animating principle that functions as an "ego," as a "self." Contemporary thought has eliminated *pneuma* but retained *psyche*. Thus "psychology" is a science and a therapy, addressed to the variable and subjective psyche within. It is a science that, in its secular manifestation, treats the human subject by neutralizing the most significant characteristic of that subject, namely its relationship to the Divine.

In the modern scheme, the spirit proper is by definition absent, along with its transcendent principle. The only self, the only principle, remaining within the machine is—as indicated above—the inconstant and turbulent psyche, opening "down" to the subconscious and the body and "up" to an apparent void. It is this remnant of self that is "adjusted" by the skillful therapist; this "lesser self" whose unsteady and discordant elements are harmonized (or so it is hoped) in relation to one another and to the surrounding milieu.

By contrast, the traditional view admits the transcendent principle of spirit. Spirit and soul are viewed as separate and substantive entities in their own right. Each has its assigned roles. This understanding goes beyond esoterist speculation; it is revelation, "from above," as noted previously. St. Paul speaks of the God of peace as sanctifying the person "wholly," in *spirit, soul* and *body* (1 Thessalonians 5:23). Recovery of this neglected knowledge is vital if we are to understand ourselves—and the Divine—as we should. Self-knowledge and knowledge of God are inseparable. Yet the mixing of spirit and soul leads only to confusion.

So what is spirit? It is that faculty of the human person that is potentially open to the Divine. The word, in fact, emphasizes direct relationship between the individual and God. According to Holy Scripture, it was the Spirit of God, present at the beginning, that infused the "breath of life" into the dust of primordial man, thus creating a "living soul."

In his spirit, man is imbued with an intellect (or intuition), conscience, and ability to commune with God. (Artistic inspiration, aesthetic sensibility, symbolic imagination, creativity and a sense of wholeness are among the gifts which flow from intuition and the exercise of communion, as are the oft recited "gifts of the Spirit" listed in 1 Corinthians 12: wisdom, knowledge, faith, healing, miracles, prophecy, discernment, speaking in tongues and interpretation of tongues). Although the Spirit of God and the human spirit are distinguished (Romans 8:16), God's Spirit is able to infuse Himself into the receptive human spirit.

There is a proper order and harmony to the person **(see diagram four),** with the spirit assigned to govern the soul, the soul to serve the spirit, the body to incarnate the spirit and the soul, and the soul to mediate between the spirit and the body. (The manifold action of the

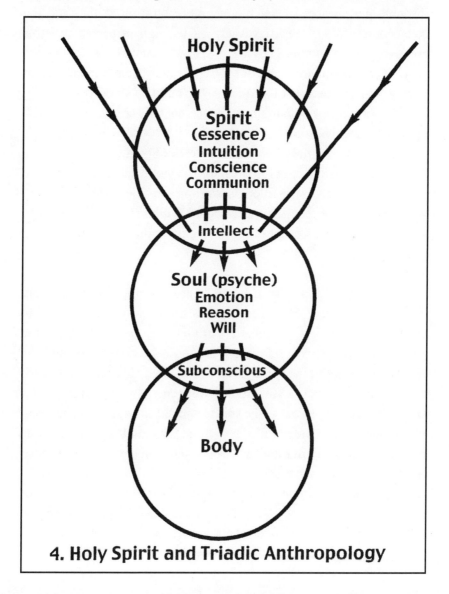

4. Holy Spirit and Triadic Anthropology

Holy Spirit, and His influence on all aspects of the tripartite person, is indicated in the diagram also). The soul animates the body in distinctive ways; it expresses individual personality, it is "who we are" in confronting the circumstances of life.

The human spirit, in its relations with God, ranges over a wide spectrum of human potential. In the domain of art, to cite one example, divine influence has long been recognized by traditional peoples. The Greeks, for instance, were wise in attributing inspiration to the Muses, the nine patronesses of the literary arts, intuiting as they did the connection between human creativity and its origin in the inexhaustible creativity of the Divine. They were wise, too, in making Apollo "the god both of imagination and of sanity; for he was both the patron of poetry and the patron of healing."[103] Thus the streams of Spirit, working through the human spirit, shower not only creativity but health upon the receptive soul.

Receptivity is vital. An openness to the Spirit and its gifts is a necessity. If this openness is present, Divine influences are able to enter the soul. The Spirit-filled human spirit is able to infuse the soul with, for instance, poetic inspiration or symbolic imagination. The spirit enriches the faculties of the soul, enlivening its willing, feeling and thinking.

In the primordial human being, there was (according to Holy Scripture and other sacred traditions) a harmony of essence and existence. In the first two chapters of Genesis, the intellect (not the profane reason, as will be discussed later), the conscience and the ability to commune with the Divine (the three aspects of the spirit which are discussed in this book), were in right relationship with God. The soul, as servant of the spirit, enjoyed an equivalent harmony of thought, emotion and will. The soul in turn guided the body in its proper functions. All of these, working together in harmony, performed their assigned roles in perfect freedom.

The great catastrophe, the primal sin, "the Fall," brought all of this to a close. The fruit of the Tree of the Knowledge of Good and Evil was preferred to the Tree of Life. As a consequence, our earliest

---

[103] G. K. Chesterton, *Orthodoxy*, p. 29

ancestors were expelled from their lush and shady bower, into the world of intractable nature, of thorns and thistles, of travail in childbirth and painful toil; the world of alienation, exile and dissimilarity. As a result, the Spirit withdrew from the human spirit, the previous harmony between Divine and human was ruptured. The cherubim were assigned (with "flaming sword") to bar re-entry to the Garden and its Tree of Life. The spirit had been severed from its divine root.*

With the spirit virtually dead, the soul experienced an inflation of importance. No longer a servant, the soul became a law unto itself. The mind, finite and autonomous, became ever-restless, ever-questioning; the emotions, disordered and inordinate; the will, willful and misdirected. The residues of spirit were consumed by soul. In subsequent ages, God's Word (incarnate and written)—as made manifest by His Spirit—would become the only means to rightly divide spirit and soul, to pierce the division between them, to redeem the one and heal the other.

Spiritual influences, however, have not come solely from above. Humankind was not alone in revolt nor was it first in revolt. An earlier rebellion had occurred in "the heavenlies" and the alienated spirits from that conflict have ever since served as tempters to unredeemed man. Certain men and women were—and are—able to channel these spirits "from below." Thus one encounters the figure of the spiritualist, the occultist, the dark magician. Open not to the Holy Spirit but to the infernal spirits, this diabolical line seeks generation after generation to return to the primal glory, employing as it does the techniques of inversion—and ever failing to reach its goal.

For most persons, such Promethean strivings in the subterranean world are of no interest. Their sins are, by contrast, "human, all too human." Their sins are "of the flesh" and, as such, reflect the everyday dominance of the soul and the marginalization of the spirit. No better illustration can be found than St. Paul's discourse in Romans 7. In that passage there is a vivid presentation of the spirit-soul divide, of the soul's work though the "members" of the body, of the presence of indwelling sin even in the redeemed. The passage makes clear the necessity of "spiritual warfare," of the inner conflict that challenges to engagement all serious Christians, as well as others who follow a related path. (In Islam, for instance, the "Lesser Jihad" concerns itself with outer battles while the *"Greater* Jihad" addresses the *inner* conflict).

In Romans 7, the apostle confesses his understanding and approval of the good he would like to do, of the better way he would like to follow, even as he chooses the worse. Thus, in Paul's divided consciousness, the spiritual and the carnal are pitted against one another. The real, authentic self honors the ideal, the good, the law. Sin, however, active in the lower nature, drags the self to where it does not wish to go.

"I do not understand what I do," Paul confesses. "For what I want to do, I do not do, but what I hate I do." (v. 15). He continues: "As it is, it is no longer I myself who do it, but it is sin living in me." (v. 17). Paul sums up his dilemma of double-mindedness in verses 21-23: "So I find this law at work: When I want to do good, evil is right there with me. For in my inner being I delight in God's law; but I see another law at work in the members of my body, waging war against the law of my mind and making me a prisoner of the law of sin at work within my members."

The "inner being" ("inner" from the Greek, "eso," the root of esoteric, esoterist and related words) and the "mind" (from "nous," the divine or human intellect) to which Paul refers are equivalent to his spirit. The "inner being" is his highest self. It is this spirit that is in tension with the restless and recalcitrant soul and with the soul's materialization in bodily deeds. It is this split that needs to be healed.

In the words of James Denney, "To be saved from sin a man must at the same time own it and disown it; it is this practical paradox which is reflected in [verse 21]."[104] The Enneagram addresses this "practical paradox" in a unique and effective way.

* We here append a rather lengthy but not unneccessary comment on the question of human origins. In doing so we point out the incongruity between the profane and the sacred views of human origins. This is

---

[104] *The New Bible Commentary,* p. 1029

not a matter of indifference. In the data of "the Fall" that is summarized above, the Hebrew account of origins is employed. By using this account, one escapes the insufficiency of the profane point of view, a point of view that is not only limited in explanatory power but that is arguably false. It is a view that absolutizes the mundane and the natural at the expense of the sacred and the supernatural. It reduces "the real" to the confines of the material realm, to the realm of the empirically knowable.

In this view, the Mythos of the Evolution of Man undergirds the prejudices of the contemporary mindset. Darwinism and its variant successors and promulgators have left to the world of intellect and reason and, ultimately, to the world of everyday discourse a legacy of theoretical and practical randomness and incoherence. Additionally, it has left to the world the promise of a limited and temporal salvation from below (to be experienced in the posture of heroic despair) in place of an enduring salvation from above. By contrast, the Mythos of the Divinely Created Man is a view that is compatible with the existential facts of the human condition as well as the universal testimony of the race.

By the Mythos of the Divinely Created Man is meant the understanding of the creation that is common in one way or another to the sacred literatures of nearly all peoples. It is a story told in a hundred ways in a hundred myths, in a hundred refractions of the Primordial Tradition as it spread and divided among the scattering inhabitants of the earth, but it is a story congruent with the spiritual and psychological realities of the race. The many myths of a vanished Golden Age and subsequent prophecies of restoration attest to the Fall and Redemption of the race, not to its evolution and futility.

The creature we know as man was once a nobler figure than the wounded being we encounter on a daily basis and into whose depths we can peer by the art of introspection. In the view of Frithjof Schuon, "Original man was not a simian being barely capable of speaking and standing upright; he was a quasi-immaterial being enclosed in an aura still celestial, but deposited on earth."[105] This speculation is congruent with the account in Genesis, wherein man is described as a being into

---

[105] *To Have a Center*, p. 50

whom God breathed his own breath, or spirit, at which point man (who was materially of the earth) became a "living soul."

This being of ages past was in close proximity spiritually to the celestial realm, to the transcendent realities and the Transcendent Being that are in this day so seemingly distant. Sacred History as revealed in the Bible, which tells of these earliest ages, can be divided into three essential phases: the metahistorical, from the origin to the fall of Adam; the parahistorical, from the Fall to the Tower of Babel, and the historical, starting with Abraham.[106] Thus in the earliest narratives one reads of the Creation, of man in Paradise, of the Fall, and of the Exile from Paradise, all of which are clothed in symbol and allegory but are not necessarily "mythical" in their entirety. Elements of the historical (even though space and time may indeed have been constituted differently than in today's world and even though the imagination of today finds it hard to grasp such distant events) cannot be ruled out. In fact, the seamless sequence of events in the first 11 chapters of Genesis and their transition into the ever more transparently "real" argues for a measure of historicity, no matter how wondrously strange that history may seem to us now.

It is in this Sacred History that one finds the keys to the mystery of man. It is in these earliest narratives that one finds a being who can inspire endless speculation. For here is a primal being with an inherent wholeness, an innate but embryonic understanding of the arts and sciences, an ability to communicate with the Divine. Here is a being with the favor of the Divine resting upon him and with a companion given to him to complement his every happiness. Yet this man and this woman, given the freedom to choose, chose wrongly. Their fall was followed by their exile, even as the gates of Paradise, which guarded the Tree of Life, were barred to them.

Thus began a declension of the race at a point very near its origins. Subsequent generations retained mere fragments of the primeval unity and dignity. Man's unruly thoughts, feelings and desires became the stuff of history, that "collection of the crimes, follies, and misfortunes" of mankind (Voltaire). The Enneagram, which peers into the inner

---

[106] These phases are suggested by Jean Borella in his *The Sense of the Supernatural*, p. 101

workings of the fallen psyche, maps this disharmony and imbalance, these passions and weaknesses of the soul. Yet it is not the adroit use of the Enneagram that sets right the things which have gone so wrong. The Enneagram describes, it does not cure. It points the way to understanding, it does not provide the power of transformation. Rather, according to Sacred History, it is the Redeeming Blood that reconciles the inner and outer discord of the wayward members of the race, that knits together the fallen creatures who carry in their inmost being the weight of the primordial castastrophe, and that puts these fallen creatures once again in right relationship with the Divine.

14

The Spirit and Its Faculties

*"Spirit, and Soul, and Body, the man consisting of
neither separately, but of the whole three together."*
—E. W. Bullinger

It cannot be stressed too much that spirit and soul are not the same
thing. This vital piece of knowledge, however, remains obscured
or denied in the modern age. Theology and philosophy, inasmuch as
they are influenced by the extended shadow of Descartes and his
dualistic view of man (as well as a whole raft of later materialist
assumptions) perpetuate the error.

In this view, everything that is not material, that is not identified
as part of the body of man, is conflated into a single non-corporeal
entity called "soul" or "spirit," it matters not which. Thus the "vertical"
qualities of spirit are confused with the "horizontal" functions of soul.
The result is a distinct and harmful loss of understanding, with "spirit"
trivialized and indifferently applied to the emotions ("high spirits")
and the will power (a "spirited" defense) and even inanimate
substances (alcoholic "spirits").*

As shown in the previous chapter, human beings possess spirit as
an instrinsic part of their nature. "The Lord... forms the spirit of man
within him" (Zechariah 12:1). The human spirit is distinguished from
the soul and from the Holy Spirit. The spirit (or "essence") is the
organ of intuitive communication with God, of relationship with Him

at the profoundest levels. It accounts for the "sense of deity" intrinsic to all men. By contrast, the soul (or psyche), with its reason, emotion and will, does not enter directly into this communication. In fact, subject as it is to the distortion of sin and compulsion, the soul is an impediment to this communication, interrupting the human spirit in its intended relations with the Holy Spirit. The Enneagram, as will be seen, addresses these distortions in detail and in depth, opening channels through which the spirit can flow into the soul. **

The human spirit has three interrelated elements **(see diagram five)**: intellect (or intuition), conscience, and the ability to commune with the transcendental realm (communion). The first of the triad, intellect, is not to be confused with profane reason, which is found in the mind (which, again, is part of the soul). The intellect, rather, is the

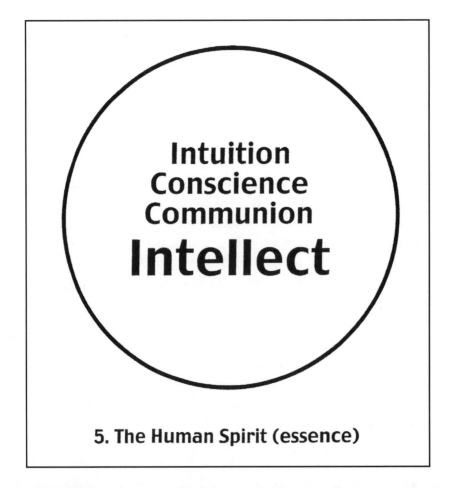

Intuition
Conscience
Communion
Intellect

5. The Human Spirit (essence)

foundation of the human spirit. It is the conduit to the divine. "He put his own light into their hearts to show them the magnificence of his works" (Ecclesiastes 17:8). Owing, however, to the distortions of an unhealthy soul, the pure light of the Holy Spirit does not shine unhindered into the human spirit. The way is impeded by bondages and blockages in the personality patterns that vary from individual to individual. Even so, the believer is receptive to the Spirit of God to one degree or another, within the constraints of individual temperament, habit... and sin. Thus the mature Christian can agree with St. Paul: "We do not have the spirit of the world but the Spirit who is from God" (1 Corinthians 2:12).

Only God can reveal the truth of the Gospel to the intellect and only then to the willing recipient. "The man without the Spirit does not accept the things that come from the Spirit of God, for they are foolishness to him, and he cannot understand them, because they are spiritually discerned" (1 Corinthians 2:14). Many persons are manifestly unable to receive the things of the Spirit. They are blind; they have not "eyes to see." No sequence of logical deductions can prove to them that God exists or that He is identifiable by particular attributes or activities. Their inmost being remains untouched by grace, they cannot discern spiritually. They are, as a result, indifferent and sometimes hostile to the things of God. "The fool says in his heart there is no God" (Psalm 14:1). By contrast, once a person is enlightened by the Spirit of God at work in the intellect, that person is aware of the workings of the spiritual world, is brought into an abiding awareness of God, is able to search "even the deep things of God" (1 Corinthians 2:10).

The contrast between intellect and reason is addressed by C. S. Lewis in *The Discarded Image,*[107] wherein he notes that Samuel Taylor ' placed "understanding" (by which the poet meant the equivalent of intellect) below "reason." In this, Coleridge was a modern, inverting as he did the nature of things. By contrast, Lewis explains, Boethius (writing in the sunset of antiquity) distinguished the two, *intelligentia* from *ratio* (the former enjoyed in its perfection by angels) and placed them in the proper vertical order.

---

[107] p. 157

According to Lewis, *intellectus* is that in man which is closest to the angelic *intelligentia*, a capability that appropriates without exertion. He draws on Aquinas to show its relation to reason: "Intellect... is the simple... grasp of an intelligible truth, whereas reasoning... is the progression towards an intelligible truth by going from one understood... point to another. The difference between them is thus like the difference between rest and motion or between possession and acquisition."[108] Thus one experiences the activity of the intellect when one simply "sees" a self-evident truth (hence the "intuitive" sense of this faculty) as opposed to the step-by-step processes of the profane reason. This potential "seeing," this "sense of deity," is embryonic in all persons, engraved on their hearts but obscured by sin.

Truth is "in the inner parts... in the inmost place" (Psalm. 51:6). It is, in traditional language, through "the eye of the heart" that one sees spiritual truths. This is why St. Augustine could call for "the healing of the inner eye of man," or St. Paul could ask that "the eyes of your heart" be opened to see the light (Ephesians 1:18). Jesus Christ, too, in the Sermon on the Mount, called blessed "the pure in *heart*, for they shall *see* God" (Matthew 5:8, italics added). This "eye" is the symbol of the organ that takes in the "light" of truth. It is the symbol of the intellect, of the faculty that is the conduit of metaphysical truth.

As the Holy Spirit works as an inward witness in the human spirit, the intellect is revitalized and opened to divine truth. To the one thus opened, the Holy Scriptures, which before had been seen as human artifacts—as the legends and speculations and heavily edited history of pious souls—are transformed by varying degrees into the light and truth of God. The holy things judged "from below" and dismissed earlier are now acknowledged as coming "from above." The Word Written (Scripture)—as well as The Word Incarnate (Jesus Christ)— begins to penetrate and permeate the receptive heart. The believer begins to take in the Holy Words, to "eat them" as Ezekiel ate the scroll from God ("and it tasted as sweet as honey"). The believer, inspired by the inner witness, "learns, marks, studies and inwardly

---

[108] Ibid., p. 157

digests" the scriptures (as the Anglican collect puts it). The Bible comes to be viewed through the eyes of the heart, as verbal expression alive with God's inspiration.

The human subject, at this point, begins to settle into a stable inner peace, increasingly content amidst the principial and archetypal truths, amidst the truths "which prefigure and determine all others."[109] It is this intuitive yet objective appropriation of truth that is the gift of God by way of the intellect, the conduit of the Holy Spirit. In Luther's words, "The Holy Spirit is no Sceptic, and the things He has written in our hearts are not doubts or opinions, but assertions—surer and more certain than sense and life itself."[110]

This truth, according to 1 Corinthians 2:6, is "not the wisdom of this age or of the rulers of this age." It is "God's secret wisdom, a wisdom that has been hidden and that God destined for our glory before time began." (v. 7). It is wisdom hidden not only from the unbeliever but from the "baby" Christian or the slothful or careless Christian, for whom milk and not solid food is the prescribed diet.

The second faculty of the human spirit to be examined is conscience, wherein is located the ability to tell right from wrong. Unlike intellect, which is opaque to the modern mentality, conscience is something of which the average person is well aware, especially in cases of bad conscience. It is the stab of guilt, the nagging regret, that makes one aware of doing wrong and of the need to make amends. "Remorse begets reform" (William Cowper). Conscience is aware of right and wrong because of its link to the Holy Spirit, whose mission it is (in part) to enlighten the human spirit ethically.

The conscience accuses (or excuses) within a relationship to the soul. The soul, for its part, tends to employ its reason, emotion and will to channel the promptings of conscience along the course of selfish motives. Thus the mind can be put to use to reason away an evil deed, as in "situation ethics." The feelings, too, can assuage guilt ("It *felt* like the right thing to do."). The intentions can be recruited, as well. ("I *meant* it for good; how was I to know?").

---

[109] Frithjof Schuon, *Survey of Metaphysics and Esoterism*, p. 3
[110] John Dillenberger, *Martin Luther, Selections From His Writings*, p. 171

Owing to its relationship to soul, one can have a tender conscience, a coarsened conscience, or no conscience at all. Temperament, habit and upbringing form the patterns of the conscience. The conscience, working as it does through the soul, cannot express itself on right and wrong in detached purity. Take a man raised in the Jewish faith who converts to Christianity. As a Christian, he will know that he is free to eat pork and other foods that Jewish dietary laws forbid. Even so, his conscience revolts at the thought of eating pork. No amount of reasoning can ease his mind in the matter. St. Paul understood and empathized with such a conflicted state (in his letter to the Romans, in regard to eating meat that had been sacrificed to idols), warning that conscience should not be violated in such matters, regardless of what reason or religious knowledge indicate. "But the man who has doubts is condemned if he eats, because his eating is not from faith; and everything that does not come from faith is sin" (14:23).

Any number of scriptures can be cited in reference to issues of conscience. For example:

"I still had no peace of mind" (2 Corinthians 2:13).

"Have mercy on me, O God, according to your unfailing love; according to your great compassion blot out my transgressions. Wash away all my iniquity and cleanse me from my sin. For I know my transgressions, and my sin is always before me. Against you, you only, have I sinned and done what is evil in your sight, so that you are proved right when you speak and justified when you judge" (Psalm 51:1-4).

"Create in me a pure heart, O God, and renew a steadfast spirit within me" (Psalm 51:10).

"For day and night your hand was heavy upon me; my strength was sapped as in the heat of summer. Then I acknowledged my sin to you and did not cover up my iniquity. I said, 'I will confess my transgressions to the LORD'—and you forgave the guilt of my sin" (Psalm 32: 4-5).

"The Lord is close to the brokenhearted and saves those who are crushed in spirit" (Psalm 34:18).

"Let us draw near to God with a sincere heart in full assurance of faith, having our hearts sprinkled to cleanse us from a guilty conscience" (Hebrews 10:22).

"So I strive always to keep my conscience clear before God and man" (Acts 24:16).

"But do this with gentleness and respect, keeping a clear conscience" (I Peter 3: 15-16).

To live with a clear conscience, to be free from the pangs of remorse, is a great blessing. Such a blessing comes to a life lived "in the spirit;" lived in obedience, self knowledge, humility and repentance.

"No one knows what he is doing so long as he is acting rightly; but of what is wrong one is always conscious." (Goethe). To act rightly: this is another key to a clear conscience. Good habits, established and maintained, lead to a "carefree" life in the healthy sense of that word, to a life that bears the fruit of the spirit, against which there is no law.

The third faculty of the human spirit to be examined is the element that "communes" with the Divine. The faculty of "communion" is devoted to "worship"—in the narrower and broader senses of the word—of God. Its function, which overlaps to some extent that of the intellect, allows communication with the divine realm by means of intuition.

True communion with God is not possible to the unregenerate, to those who have not been reborn "of water and the spirit"—nor to the believer who is reborn but does not direct his spirit to this end. The reborn spirit must be opened to God at its deepest levels. "The man without the Spirit does not accept the things that come from the Spirit of God, for they are foolishness to him, and he cannot understand them, because they are spiritually discerned" (1 Corinthians 2:14). The believer needs to pray for a quickening of the spirit, so that God may give "the Spirit of wisdom and revelation, so that you may know him better" (Ephesians 1:17). The person who prays needs to be sensitive to the Holy Spirit's signs, to His promptings, revelations and answers to prayer. Faith and submission are required, as are openness, obedience and humility. And one must "discern the spirits," to determine if they are from "above" or "below."

The Bible speaks of communing with God through worship formally and informally, often with a stress on interior relationship, in numerous passages:

"The true worshippers will worship the Father in spirit and truth" (John 4:23).

"And my spirit rejoices in God my Savior" (Luke 1:47).

"She had a sister called Mary, who sat at the Lord's feet listening to what he said... "but only one thing is needed. Mary has chosen what is better'" (Luke 10:39, 42).

"For you did not receive a spirit that makes you a slave again to fear, but you received the Spirit of sonship" (Romans 8:15).

"Do you not know that your body is a temple of the Holy Spirit, who is in you, whom you have received from God...Therefore honor God with your body" (1 Corinthians 6:19-20).

"The Spirit himself testifies with our spirit that we are God's children" (Romans 8:16).

"But he who unites himself with the Lord is one with him in spirit" (1 Corinthians 6:17).

"So what shall I do? I will pray with my spirit, but I will also pray with my mind; I will sing with my spirit, but I will also sing with my mind" (1 Corinthians 14:15).

"And he carried me away in the Spirit to a mountain great and high, and showed me... Jerusalem, coming down out of heaven from God" (Revelation 21:10).

Thus the spirit, in its parts, is distinct from the soul. But to the soul we now turn: to the "lesser self," to the "ego," to an examination of the functions of thinking, feeling and willing.

* This last usage is not without significance. In a 1961 letter to Bill Wilson, founder of Alcoholics Anonymous, C. G. Jung touched on the connection between "spirituality" and "alcoholic spirits." According to Jung, the latter can serve as a perverse substitute for the former. When a person is spiritually empty, Jung observes, he or she is inclined to resort to "spirits" to attain a sought-after inner peace, however fleeting it may be. "You see," Jung writes, "alcohol in Latin is *spiritus* and you use the same word for the highest religious experience as well as for the most depraving poison. The helpful formula therefore is: *spiritus contra spiritum.*"[111] Religious practice is able by the gift of grace to deliver real inner peace but not as quickly as the false substitute—be it alcoholic or narcotic—and not without inner work.

** The triadic view of man employed here, its origins, variations and proponents, is examined exhaustively by a sympathetic commentator, the late Cardinal Henri de Lubac, in an essay entitled "Tripartite Anthropology" in his book, *Theology in History*.[112] Father de Lubac finds the tripartite view to be deeply rooted in scripture (as indicated by St. Paul's reference in 1 Thessalonians 5:23 but elsewhere as well). He maintains the doctrine is Biblical and Semitic, not Greek. Philo (a little earlier than Paul), he observes, although friendly to Hellenism, speaks of God breathing "pneuma" (spirit) into man at the creation rather than *nous*, nous being the term used by Aristotle for the superior element in man (*nous* as the principal of intellectual life, immortal and divine). "This *pneuma*, in man, is the principle of a higher life, the place of communication with God. Now such is also one of the meanings of pneuma in Saint Paul. It is not in Greece that we must search for its origin but in the Bible."[113]

In the early centuries of the post-Biblical period, Father de Lubac shows, one finds the tripartite anthropology in Irenaeus, Origen, Evagrius Ponticus and Augustine. In subsequent centuries, it appears

---

[111] Gerhard Adler, editor, in collaboration with Aniela Jaffé, *C. G. Jung: Letters,* p. 625
[112] pp. 117-200
[113] Ibid. p. 125

in Gregory the Great, John Scotus, William of St. Thierry, Bonaventure, Aquinas, Tauler, Nicholas of Cusa, Teresa of Avila and Francis de Sales, as well as many others. During the Reformation period and later, it can be found in Erasmus, Luther, Calvin, Paracelsus (in the hermetic line), Tersteegan and the Anglican Lancelot Andrews. In this century, the Lutherans Bonhoeffer and Ole Hallesby have drawn upon its riches, as have the Catholics Paul Claudel, Georges Bernanos and, at the present time, Jean Borella.

One can also find the doctrine expounded by numerous proponents of the holiness and charismatic traditions, among them Otto Stockmayer, Andrew Murray, F. B. Meyer, Watchman Nee, Derek Prince and Dennis and Rita Bennett.

15

Types and Triads

"Your soul accomplishes very little even though
it always appears busy."
—Madame Guyon

T he human spirit (or "essence") is potentially in contact with the
Holy Spirit (or "Divine Essence"). This is so because human
beings are created in the image of God. In the beginning, Creator and
creature enjoyed an Edenic affinity. Since the Fall, however,
communion has been severed. Human beings, barred from the Tree
of Life, have become the orphans of the universe, exiles from essence.

In their fallen condition, men and women are bound to "the wheel
of existence" (James 3:6, *New English Bible*). On the wheel as on the
Enneagram circle—with its nine points of false integration—they are
subject to a "vanity of vanities." Cycles of birth and death, rise and
fall, gain and loss repeat themselves. "What has been will be again,
what has been done will be done again; there is nothing new under
the sun" (Ecclesiastes 1:9). It is a world of despair, ever-revolving,
ever repeating. It is a world of the coiled serpent, of the closed circle
without exit. Exiles bound to the wheel are helpless to escape. They
stand in need of both liberator and mediator, of Him who will free the
captives and reestablish the conduit between human and Divine, of
Him who will rebind, as it were, heaven and earth.

That mediator is Jesus Christ who, obedient to the Father, died an atoning death for his people. Thus the liberation and the rebinding have begun. Following Christ's Crucifixion, Resurrection and Ascension, the Holy Spirit descended in fiery tongues upon the disciples. That Spirit, which kindled the flame that became the church, is still active in the "twice-born" human spirit, illuminating the human soul, bringing balance, integration, peace, power and purpose.

The attainment by any given individual of such a happy state is far from guaranteed. Though one be regenerated in one's spirit, the soul—the seat of personality and the organ of consciousness—remains bound to the wheel of existence. In attempting escape in its own strength, the soul seeks means to happiness that render it unhappy. It needs to be unblocked from a host of impediments and destructive patterns to allow the renewed spirit to do its work. The baggage of a lifetime, the burden of sins, bad choices, obsessions, compulsions, stresses and strains, must be addressed.

The life of sanctification has to be walked, knowing all along that God is working within and without, in harmony, with purpose, to bring the believer to deliverance and completion. "The potter has in his mind's eye a beautiful image which he would reproduce, and he molds it on the wheel which is before him, and if it is yielding and plastic the result is as he wishes. But if the clay is refractory, the vessel is marred—all of which means that God will not do violence to the will of man."[114]

In this sacred commerce the soul treats with God and no other. Ceremonialism apart from knowledge will not suffice, the relationship must be personal, open, accepting. One's "clay" must be yielding not refractory. There is no proxy salvation; heart commitment is required. "Self-realization through Christ is the end."[115]

The Enneagram provides a symbolic framework of the soul, a nine-point arrangement in which healthy and unhealthy characteristics are catalogued. The nine types are, in turn, placed within the triads of emotion, mind and will (or heart, head and belly), triads in which the special preoccupations and issues—for good or ill—of the nine types can be analyzed.

---

[114] E. Y. Mullins, *The Axions of Religion,* p. 90
[115] Ibid., p. 51

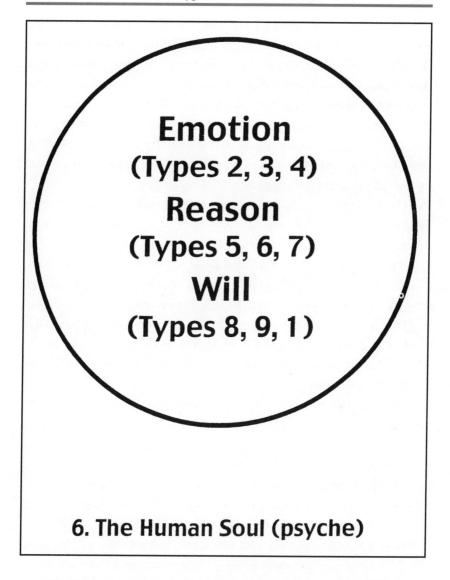

Emotion
(Types 2, 3, 4)
Reason
(Types 5, 6, 7)
Will
(Types 8, 9, 1)

6. The Human Soul (psyche)

The types in each triad **(see diagram six)** share key elements of personality, as follows: The Two, Three and Four are in the Triad of the Emotions; the Five, Six and Seven, the Triad of the Mind, and the Eight, Nine and One, the Triad of the Will. This is not to say that the faculties of emotion, mind and will are isolated within these triads and nowhere else, only that they are the predominating and defining characteristics of the types in their triad.

The types in the Triad of the Emotions (the Twos, Threes and Fours) are centered on an affective state of consciousness. To them, the feelings—pleasure, pain, joy, sorrow, fear, hate, love, anger, dejection, bliss—are paramount. Good feelings are vital in making their lives worth living. They remember, enjoy and anticipate good feelings. Feelings are the principal link with other persons, the cosmos and God. Personal relationships and sensitivity to others, based on these feelings, are key aspects of the core self. Feelings are experienced as the seat of spiritual intuition.

The importance of this triad to true humanness is touched upon by C. S. Lewis in his *Abolition of Man,*[116] wherein he draws on traditional ideas to convey the mediating role of the emotions. "The Chest—Magnanimity—Sentiment—these are the indispensable liaison officers between cerebral man and visceral man." Lewis feared that modern thought and educational theory were producing "Men without Chests," thus fashioning a spirit or an animal but not a complete human being. The Enneagram, with its inclusion of the "chest" (or the "heart," midway between the head and the belly) allows for the fully human.

The "heart," however, must be harmonized with the other two triads. To mature, members of this triad must learn that their emotions are not, in and of themselves, guides to right conduct. Their feelings have to be from time to time overridden, sometimes frequently. The strongest emotion always clamors for precedence, be it anger, lust or fear. Even "good" emotions, love or pity, can be applied at the wrong time or place. Discernment needs to be exercised.

In addition to enjoying pleasant emotions, members of the triad need to learn to face unpleasant emotions, as well. The ability to counter such emotions, control them or, in some cases, simply endure them, is a requirement of adult living. In this, faith is indispensable. "Cast all your anxiety on him because he cares for you" (1 Peter 5:7). Faith, in the sense of trust, needs to be exercised on a day-to-day basis. "For you will keep in perfect peace him whose mind is steadfast because he trusts in you" (Isaiah 26:3).

The natural affections, kept in bounds, are among God's greatest

---

[116] p. 34

gifts. The loves defined by the Greeks cover the range of territory especially claimed by the Triad of the Emotions. Affection, of parents towards offspring and offspring towards parents, or between siblings, old friends or acquaintances, or between pets and their masters, define an important part of the triad's felt concern. So, too, do other loves: friendship, with its devotion to shared experiences, hobbies and tastes; eros, with its sexual and romantic longings, and charity, or "agape," with its love of the unloveable.

In this triad, Type Twos direct their emotions at others, investing themselves in others and the issues that concern them. They "live for others," doing good to them in the hope that they will succeed, by such a strategy, in making *themselves* feel good, in making themselves loved.

Type Threes are disconnected from their emotions. Their emotions are important, as it were, because of their apparent absence. Threes may seem responsive on the surface but deeper feelings are kept in check, all the better to approach life with a focused striving, unhindered by emotional ups and downs.

Type Fours direct their emotions at themselves. They seek self-fulfillment through emotional intensity. They live and die with their emotional states, first up, then down. They are beset by a temptation to loathe themselves and to bemoan their circumstances. "I loathe my life; therefore I will give free rein to my complaint" (Job 10:1).

The types in the Triad of the Mind are centered on thinking, on the faculty whereby they know and understand. By placing supreme worth in their mental functions, members of this triad seek to comprehend things both great and small, from daily encounters and their significance to the cosmos and its meaning. They are compelled to understand all things, to find an explanation for every detail, and to place their observations into an over-arching theory. If something cannot be grasped by the mind, their own or others, it is repelled from the borders of consciousness. Such unwanted realities may be "out of sight, out of mind" but they are present nonetheless, seeking integration into the total being.

Members of the triad ("head types") get into trouble when they rely to an unwarranted degree upon the powers of reason. The consuming faculty of reason and its tool, logic, can render the richness of creation a mere abstraction. The impersonal and clinical view can reduce, seemingly—but only seemingly—all of reality to a manageable affair, a condition much desired by the person solely reliant upon the powers of thought.

The prideful thinker thinks (in his view) autonomously in a universe devoid of meaning, unaware of transcendental realities. Here the mind does not serve the eyes of understanding, through which essence and existence are perceived and interpreted, but becomes an object of idolatry, an end in itself. With no ultimately serious object upon which to exercise itself, the mind becomes a player of games and a creator of theories in the void.

The mind, turned in upon itself, is closed to the aspects of reality which bypass the discursive processes. The world of intuition is barred from playing a role. Such a state is but partially human. It is the Spirit and the divine words that quicken the soul, that give life (John 6:63). The human spirit, influenced by that which transcends spirit, enriches and guides the soul.

Reasoning in the void can never attain a state of certainty. The solution of a problem only makes way for the posing of another. Today's certainty is confounded by tomorrow's doubt. Without faith (trust) in the Creator, there is no solution to the intellectual problems that plague the restless mind.

In God's order, Christ is the center; the reasoning mind an instrument to serve that center. In the words of St. Paul: "We demolish arguments and every pretension that sets itself up against the knowledge of God, and we take captive every thought to make it obedient to Christ" (2 Corinthians 10:5). When the Divine is at the center, "Wisdom will enter your heart, and knowledge will be pleasant to your soul" (Proverbs 2:10).

In this triad, Type Fives display a pride of intellect. By amassing facts and devising theories, they seek a safe haven within a threatening environment. The inner castle, built of complex and systematic formulations, is their bulwark against the insults of life.

Type Sixes are subject to the world of thought, as well, but their mode of thought (obsessive and fretful) is generally characterized by a submission to the pronouncements of others. With little self-trust or disposition to think for themselves, they are disconnected from the resources of their own mind, even as they analyze keenly the mental products of others.

Type Sevens, with issues revolving about the mind, also, are characterized by a *disdain* for serious thought, even as they are "quick studies" and superficial "whizzes" in many areas of endeavor. Regardless of how high their intelligence, they have difficulty—and little apparent interest—in sustaining systematic reflection as they flit from one subject to another.

The types in the Triad of the Will, the Eights, Nines and Ones, are centered on the issues of volition and endeavor. "The will is the strong blind man who carries on his shoulders the lame man who can see." (Schopenhauer). These "gut types" make plans, take action, motivate themselves, exert themselves and strive for goals (the Nine does these things in paradoxical ways). They represent "the moving centre" in the scheme of G. I. Gurdjieff.[117] They are demanding of themselves and, in the case of the Eight, intimidating to others. They are prone to "shoulds" (especially the One).

Members of this triad measure themselves against others. They want to know who is strong, who is weak, who is right, who is wrong, who is in charge, who is subservient. They can be self-righteous as well as self-critical. They stubbornly hold to what they think is right. Also, they tend to be dissatisfied, with an underlying sense of hostility about the way things are. There is a "pressing against" reality, both internal and external.

The "gut types" have a natural bent to do things their way. In this, willpower is their chief resource. They are not interested in fitting into an overall pattern of living to which they might have been "called." Rather, they wish to shape their own destiny, to set their own agenda and timetable.

---

[117] James Moore, *Gurdjieff: A Biography,* p. 55

The types in the triad have problems with guidance, rejecting it in favor of their own instinctive sense of how to proceed. Whether seeking control of the environment, aspiring to perfect rectitude or searching for perfect peace, members of this triad employ the will according to their own lights, to serve their own ends.

God, in fact, wants believers to use their wills. After all, He created the will as a faculty of vital importance in the psyche. The will has its proper purposes. "Now devote your heart and soul to seeking the LORD your God" (1 Chronicles 22:19). The will, as such, is innocent unless perverted to sinful ends.

God does not seek the destruction or suppression of the will. He does, however, wish to see a redirecting and sanctifying of the will. "Seek first his kingdom and his righteousness and all these things will be given to you as well" (Matthew 6:33). He wishes to see human energies and passions, alive in the Spirit, redirected voluntarily towards the living of a renewed life.

Within the Triad of the Will, one can discern elements of the choleric, melancholic and phlegmatic tendencies. The will of the Eight is directed outward, with great, instinctive energy, towards mastery of the environment. Self-reliant and intent on domination, the Eight embodies a "will to power."

By contrast, of the three types, Nines are the most out of touch with their will. They, too, expend a great deal of energy but it is a suppressive energy directed inward. By this, they put the brakes on their impulse to act, an impulse that might upset a much sought-after tranquility. Their goal is stasis, the attainment of stability, peace and harmony.

Type Ones, manifesting a third variant of the triad, exercise their will both inward and outward; inward in an effort of exacting self control ("So I strive always to keep my conscience clear before God and man." Acts 24:16) and outward in an attempt to shape the environment according to their perfectionistic standards.

The unconscious **(see diagram seven),** the lowest realm of the "subtle world," falls under the purview of soul. It is that aspect of the soul that contains psychic material of which the conscious self is unaware. It is not, however, the be-all and end-all of psychological explanations, as taught by Freud and his epigoni and those who remain influenced by psychoanalytic trends.

This is not to deny the importance of the unconscious. The forces

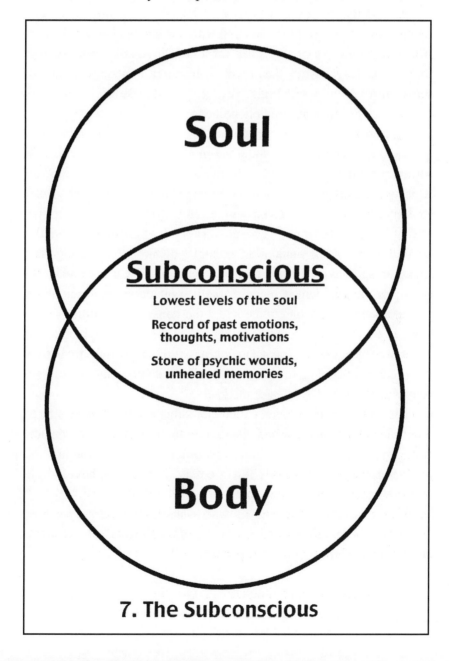

Soul

Subconscious

Lowest levels of the soul

Record of past emotions, thoughts, motivations

Store of psychic wounds, unhealed memories

Body

7. The Subconscious

of the unconscious *do* push people into emotional states and behaviors that conflict with their conscious wishes for internal peace and balanced relationships. Unhealed memories dwell in the unconscious, repressed but very much alive, influencing day-to-day life.

One need not, however, remain a passive victim of these influences. Repressed memories can be reached by prayer, introspection, counseling and the light of God's Spirit. One can open one's deepest being to the power of the Spirit through glossolalia ("speaking in tongues"), Hesychasm ("the prayer of the heart"), meditation, dream work and other disciplines, thereby gradually cleansing the unconscious of troublesome phenomena.

One must never confuse or conflate the spirit with the unconscious. To do so is to acquiesce in the great modern inversion, in which, in virtually all things, the higher is interpreted in terms of the lower. This was among the errors of C. G. Jung: the reduction of the spiritual to "psychic contents." Even worse, Jung (despite his otherwise valuable contributions) focused largely in his theories on the psychological phenomena of the mentally disturbed, confusing their dream imagery with the authentic symbolism of the transcendent. In Jung, the transcendent is reduced to "the collective unconscious," a universal entity that functions *below* the conscious faculties of the soul, even while it is used to account for the sacred symbols and other archetypes of the transcendent (a realm that thoroughly baffles the secular psychologist, if it is not discounted as a matter of course) that are *above* the faculties of the soul.

The unconscious is better called the "subconscious," according to René Guénon. "It happens that the subconscious, thanks to its contacts with psychic influences of the lowest order, succeeds in 'aping' the supraconscious."[118] Thus the lower counterfeits the higher, and the modern inversion continues apace.

Such a dynamic cannot be allowed to shape an authentic spiritual teaching, nor should its confusions be allowed to adversely affect one's understanding of the Enneagram.

---

[118] *Fundamental Symbols, The Universal Language of Sacred Science,* p. 31

16

The Body and Its Discontents

"Do you not know that your body is a temple of the Holy
Spirit, who is in you... You are not your own; you were
bought at a price. Therefore honor God with your body."
—1 Corinthians 6:19-20

One cannot safely ignore the body's relationship to soul and spirit. The Christian faith is not an ethereal faith; it is not an "angelism" in which the believer seeks to become a mind without a body. The psycho-physical constitution of man, in which the immaterial and material elements play upon one another, is a reality.

The importance and dignity of the body is taken for granted today. The body is, in fact, an obsession. There is little danger of seeing it reduced to "the tomb of the soul" as in Greek thought. It is the soul and spirit themselves that are dismissed in the modern era.

Nonetheless, a few words are in order regarding the relationship between the body and the immaterial elements. Man is tripartite, as maintained in earlier chapters, and is whole and balanced only when spirit, soul *and* body are playing their proper roles.

It is the soul, enlivened by the spirit, that provides the "form" of the body. The body is not a self-sustaining entity. Rather, the corporeal aspect of the human being—its nerves, muscles, skin, glands, hair, bones—is subject to the structuring activity of the invisible and animating principles of soul and spirit. The corporeal is mortal while the immaterial endures, to be reunited (according to Christian teaching) with a reconstituted and glorified corporeality at the terminus of history.

The body is subject to typology, as are soul and spirit. W. H. Sheldon's classic triad of types—endomorphs, mesomorphs and ectomorphs (and their blends) sheds much light on the matter. In Sheldon's teaching, endomorphy refers (in simplest terms) to a soft and plump physique, mesomorphy to a hard and muscular physique, and ectomorphy to a slender and sensitive physique. In most persons, the components are combined to various degrees, there being few "pure" types.

In addition to the type of physique, there are numerous variables—life circumstances, upbringing, ethical understanding, free will—that influence one's personality type in relation to the body.

Temperament in the endomorph tends towards slow reactions, sound sleep, relaxed movements, enjoyment of physical comfort and a pronounced love of food. The temperament of the mesomorph, by contrast, finds expression in assertion, physical adventure, competition and high-energy pursuits in general. The ectomorph, in turn, is characterized by over-sensitivity, introversion, keen imagination, shyness and nervous indigestion.

One can point to relationships between the Enneagram types and the body types, at least in a general and tentative way. Thus:

• The Two tends towards the endomorph;
• The three, the mesomorph;
• The four, the ectomorph;
• The Five, the ectomorph;
• The Six, the mesomorph;
• The Seven, the endomorph;
• The Eight, the mesomorph;
• The Nine, the endomorph, and
• The One, the ectomorph.

As the Enneagram types shade off to the types on one side or the other of their principal type number (to their "wings"), the relationships with body types (and blends of types) are affected. A

Nine (which tends towards endomorphy) with an Eight wing would, for example, embody some of the qualities of the mesomorph, while a Nine with a One wing would embody some of the qualities of the ectomorph.

Regardless of body type and its influence on temperament, the body in itself is to be honored as a part of the good creation. Though "fallen," the body retains intimations of primordial dignity and holds out promise for its eventual glorification. It is not to be denigrated as it was by ascetic pagans and medievals; to be loathed as "filthy," "food for worms" or "a sack of dung." Nor, on the other hand, is it to be idolized, as it is by modern sensualists of every stripe. Neither the hair shirt, the vigil or the fast (in its extreme forms), nor the pampering, pleasuring or perversity of the hedonist, rightly address the dignity of the body. The body, a servant of higher domains, is neither saint nor sinner. It is, in fact, more sinned against than sinning, as it is used as a vehicle for the designs of the wayward soul or, less commonly, as a playground for the spirits of inversion. The body, as a servant, needs a wise master, and that requires a balanced soul illumined by the spirit.

Inasmuch as body, soul and spirit are interconnected, the body type and its temperamental characteristics are factors in personality makeup. Thus the triad of the Two, the Seven and the Nine, owing to its endomorphic tendencies, is prone to sensuality, gluttony, sloth and their derivative passions. These types need to focus on restraint, good measure and balanced living, on disciplines to establish the "golden mean" in their lives.

The triad of the Three, the Six and the Eight tends towards the mesomorphic, thereby making great demands on the body. Pushing, risking, striving, these types pursue challenging goals. Thus they are threatened by heart trouble, strokes, accidents and other sudden dangers. To counter the overly expansive aspects of their natures, they need "to take thought," to become more reflective, to count the cost before they embark on their schemes.

With the One, the Four and the Five, one enters the triad of the ectomorph. Here one finds a preponderance of tension, fatigue, anxiety, inhibition and psychosomatic illnesses. These types stand opposite the previous types. Instead of reining in their natures, the One, the Four and the Five need to move *into* action, to give scope to their potentials, to break out of their introverted routines

All nine of the types, embodied as they are in flesh and bone, are influenced by instinctive inclinations that play a role in their varied personalities. Instinctive behavior, directed at food and sex, fight or flight, sociability or withdrawal, is innate, undergirding a pattern of tendencies and activities. The Enneagram types regulate their instinctive energies in predictable ways. The One, for instance, strives to inhibit the instincts. The Eight, by contrast, "acts out," giving free reign to the instincts. The Five is largely out of touch with the instinctive life.

The study of body types is highly inexact and yet necessary. Anyone who wishes to pursue self-knowledge needs to understand his or her body and its relations with soul and spirit. This is so because God did not create human beings as angels, "minds without bodies," but as embodied creatures whose flesh and blood reality is a part of that which is to be redeemed. God asks his followers for dedication of soul and spirit, yes, but for their body selves as well. "Dear brothers, I urge you, in view of God's mercy, to offer your bodies as living sacrifices, holy and pleasing to God, which is your spiritual worship" (Romans 12:1). Followers of Christ, in spirit, soul and body, are "bought at a price" and are therefore required to honor—and offer- themselves in all their parts.

17

The Enneagram and Transformation

*"The science of alchemy (ars alchimica) I like very well,
and indeed, it is truly the natural philosophy
of the ancients."*

—Martin Luther

According to G. I. Gurdjieff, the Enneagram is a symbolic "philosopher's stone," metaphorically equivalent to that mysterious preparation of the alchemists that goes by the same name. It is this "substance" that is used to turn base metals into precious metals, to transmute lead into gold. The Enneagram, a mysterious entity in its own right, is well suited to playing a role in the ongoing transmutation of the dross of leaden personality into the purity of a redeemed self.

"From the Christian point of view, alchemy was like a natural mirror for the revealed truths: the philosopher's stone, which turned base metals into silver and gold, is a symbol of Christ."[119]

Alchemy—including that "alchemy of personality" called the Enneagram—provides access to the interior meaning of Christian revelation. It provides, too, for a deepening of the dogmas of the Christian faith. And it provides, most importantly in this instance, a *gnosis*—an illumined way of knowing—that strips away the subjective nature of the inner person, making possible an objective look at "the

---

[119] Titus Burckhardt, *Alchemy: Science of the Cosmos, Science of the Soul*, p. 18

'I-bound' soul."[120] In this inner work, the natural forces of the soul are tamed, not destroyed. They are fitted to be servants of the spirit. And as knowledge increases, one's inner being is transmuted. By stages, the subject is liberated, unified and regenerated.

This transmutation, symbolized in the spiritual alchemy of the Enneagram, is a principle that runs through life. In nature, every living entity strives to fulfill its potential, to reach perfection. In the great, vitalist scheme of things, seeds become plants, chrysalises become butterflies, food becomes flesh. Human beings, in striving to fulfill their potential, ascend to something greater, fuller, freer... or descend to something lesser, emptier, more enslaving.

In the words of John Milton:

> *Well hast thou taught the way that might direct*
> *Our knowledge, and the scale of Nature set*
> *From center to circumference, whereon*
> *In contemplating of created things*
> *By steps we may ascend to God.*
>   (*Paradise Lost,* Book V, ll. 508 ff)

In using the Enneagram to "ascend," one is advised to practice patience, to be utterly honest with oneself and to lead a life of prayer (or *aspire* to these desiderata—the Enneagram is not unrealistic about human weaknesses). The spiritual alchemists of past centuries were serious in pursuing holy lives, knowing that technique, that process, is but part of what needs to be done. Beyond technique, the "work" is personal—but personal in a way that goes beyond the limitations of the human person. It is *transpersonal.* The work occurs within the Divine circumstance "in which we live and move and have our being." The work, to be successful, requires a sober judgment of oneself within the context of Divine realities.

"Blessed are the poor in spirit, for theirs is the kingdom of heaven" (Matthew 5:3). Those who are "poor in spirit," that is, those who are humble and aware of their brokenness and sin, those who know the cost of change and their fear of it, it is they who are open to the

---

[120] Ibid., p. 27

healing and transmuting work. It is they who are willing to undergo the stages of this inner work in the symbolic "black," "white" and "red" (*nigredo, albedo* and *rubedo*) of the alchemists, to face the sometimes painful purging of profane entanglements.

The alchemical symbols of furnace and fire indicate both the elemental forces at work within the person and the pain of purification as the dross is burned away and as previously unrealized aspects of one's being are integrated into the self. In this, the "work" is accomplished in relationship to the Divine, in a sanctifying discipline, in a synergy of nature and supernature. "Who can stand when he appears? For he will be like a refiner's fire or a launderer's soap. He will sit as a refiner and purifier of silver" (Malachi 3: 2-3). In this work, the Devil's influence is purged, Christ enters. There is death and rebirth. "For we know that our old self was crucified with him so that the body of sin might be done away with, that we should no longer be slaves to sin—because anyone who has died has been freed from sin" (Romans 6:6-7). The soul is redeemed from its bondages and is unified with the spirit (and with the *Holy* Spirit as well).

"God shall manifest himself in us, if we earnestly desire it with all humility, self-denial, losing of our souls, and being nothing in ourselves."[121] The process, as it empties the soul of its inflations, knits together the scattered elements of that same soul. There is a resolution of opposites, a balancing of forces, a reconciliation of things. There is, "in Christ," a divine unification of consciousness. "For God was pleased to have all his fullness dwell in him, and through him to reconcile to himself all things, whether things on earth or things in heaven, by making peace through his blood, shed on the cross" (Colossians 1:19-20).

Christ is Lord and Center of the universe, and the integrating soul enjoys an increased participation in His nature. In this process, the two-fold law of our nature is transcended, the poles of our being start to merge, the tensions of duality are eased. Instead of living in a subjective, sleep-walking state, helplessly pulled this way and that by disparate forces, one enjoys a new measure of freedom and

---

[121] Jacob Boehme, *Forty Questions* and *The Clavis,* p. XXXVII ["To the Reader"].

objectivity. In this the dialectic of life moves towards resolution, the opposites move towards unification. Harmony increases, discord decreases.

This dynamic has affinities with music, with a sort of Pythagorean "music of the spheres," and also with an intuition that the "inherent order" of the cosmos can be reproduced in the human soul. The Enneagram has a "music" of its own. Through its esoteric properties, through its spiritual alchemy, it is tuned to the rhythms of universal equilibrium. The Enneagram brings health to the inner being, harmony to the "octave" of the psyche. One thinks of the youthful David as he played the harp to soothe the temper of Saul (1 Samuel 16: 17-23). There is in the Enneagram a "soothing" and healing sensibility of wholeness and health—as well as a warning of their opposites—and a "mapping" of the soul's ascent and descent. The healing of David's harp was short-lived but that of the Enneagram can be sustained, so long as one is willing to explore—and make one's own—this "geography of the soul."

Jesus Christ is *the* "philosopher's stone," the cornerstone rejected by the "builders" (the chief priests and Pharisees who rejected the Gospel) but available to the spiritually needy: the one who makes possible a rearrangement of the soul's habits and energies. He is the one who is available to reconcile and unify and reintegrate those split-off parts of the inner being. He is a "medicine" available to those who ask, seek and knock; to those who are "poor in spirit," to those who allow healing balm to enter the fissures of their souls. He brings healing to those who seek to curb the pretentions that would keep them aloof and autonomous. "It is not the healthy who need a doctor, but the sick... For I have not come to call the righteous, but sinners" (Matthew 9:12-13).

We can only become open to the divine presence of the Holy Spirit by breaking the bonds of our psychic patterns, by allowing the light from above to shine into the horizontal aspects of our being, by reestablishing vertical bonds with the Creator. In using the Enneagram, our souls are illumined—and transmuted—by the uncolored light of gnosis. "This we can truly say," said Jacob Boehme, "that whatsoever is transparent, and not of a gross nature, taketh in the light, as appeareth by the water which taketh in the light, and the harsh earth doth not."[122]

In this, we find ourselves at the intersection of the cross and the crossroads, of the spirit and the soul, of the horizontal and the vertical dimensions of being. The cross radiates outward in four directions, signifying "the universal diffusion of the power and providence of him who hung upon it."[123] We are wounded in our nature but the image of God remains in us. The power and providence of the Redeemer is alive and active, healing the division between soul and spirit. The unifying essence of the Holy Spirit works within us, ready to flow forth "as springs of living water."

---

[122] *Forty Questions,* p. 5
[123] St. Gregory of Nyssa, *de resurrectione christi, oration I*

18

Integration and Distintegration

"Woe to those who call evil good and good evil, who put darkness for light and light for darkness, who put bitter for sweet and sweet for bitter."
—Isaiah 5:20

It is the permeable soul to which God's Spirit, working through the human spirit, has access. The rigid, compulsed soul is, by contrast, impermeable, locked within itself and hostile to the light. Ego reduction—the taming of the soul—creates "soul space" in which the spirit can work.

Personal transformation is an ongoing process. It is a process subtle and complex, involving the integration, to higher and more harmonious states, of the discordant elements of the personality. As the return to Eden is blocked and full ascent to the Absolute awaits the hereafter, transformation does not accomplish perfection or reach completion in this life. Even so, a greater sense of wellbeing, a greater spiritual awareness and openness, awaits those who are able to reduce the ego, even in part.

In doing so, in moving beyond the realm of the egocentric, spiritual seekers develop a heightened sense of equilibrium and harmony, of lightness and freedom, as they realize the potentials that lie within their essence. By contrast, those who follow the direction of disintegration experience a hardening of the ego. The disconsolations of the unbalanced life will in their case continue to depress and distort the personality, causing an ever more in-turned and painful existence. The spirit will remain encrusted and confined.

The Enneagram type that lies in one's direction of disintegration embodies the very aspects of personality that are most needed.[124] Although movement in that direction appears to the ego to provide a quick cure, it does not. The ego, according to Riso and Hudson, is as yet unable to deal with the aspects of personality represented by that point. It is necessary, instead, to move "against the arrow" to the point of integration. It is at that point that a person must be willing to sacrifice the unhealthy habits of the ego. This is a daunting prospect, a subjecting of oneself to a sense of insecurity and trepidation. It is "letting go." It involves experiencing aspects of the personality (the Jungian "shadow") that have been hidden and suppressed.

It is also the path to authentic freedom and a harmonious inner life. It is the path of sanctification, the means of slaying those habitual sins and behaviors that have nourished the ego and blocked the workings of the Holy Spirit. As one creates inner space in which the Spirit can work, one begins to live out one's rebirth day-by-day, with healing and wholeness increasingly in evidence.

Personal relationships are primary to the Two, and the helping of others the principal source of self-worth. Twos do not need to be told twice that "It is more blessed to give than to receive." They gain a sense of superiority as they help others. They try to be all things to all people. "Lean on me" could be their motto as they attempt to play the part of a benevolent deity.

When Twos become unbalanced, they follow the arrow **(see diagrams eight and nine for directions of disintegration and integration of the types)** to the Eight, where they take on some of the unhappy features of that type. They may seek vengeance against a significant figure in their life, someone who has spurned them or shown ingratitude. They become aggressive and manipulative and their anger rises to the surface. Their mission in life, to be loved and appreciated, is frustrated and they have come full circle, now manifesting hatred instead of love.

When Twos move towards wholeness and balance, they work

---

[124]See Don Richard Riso and Russ Hudson, *Personality Types: Using the Enneagram for Self-Discovery,* p. 415

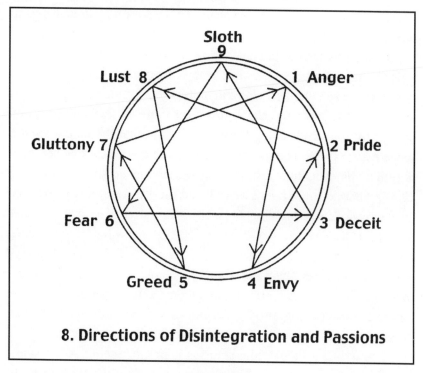

8. Directions of Disintegration and Passions

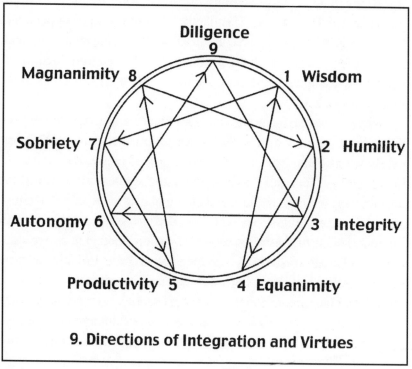

9. Directions of Integration and Virtues

against the arrow to take on the healthy attitudes of the Four. They no longer need to live by way of their self-publicized altruism, gaining their sense of worth as helpers and saviours. Like a Four, they begin to look inside, to become aware of their emotions. They are able to admit their needs, faults, pains and motivations. Pride is curbed. Twos are enabled to open to others, to reveal more of themselves. They even learn to ask for help. They realize, too, that the love and care received *from* others equips them to provide enhanced love and care *for* others. They learn true humility, to accept the perspective of Luke 17:10, wherein the diligent servants admit, "We are unworthy... we have only done our duty." A necessary—though at first unwelcome— lesson for the Two.

The Three must always appear competent, in control, successful. In short, the number Three is intent on being "Number One." In carrying out this program, Threes fall in love with their image (the image they have themselves created and cultivated in conformity with the surrounding milieu) while ignoring their inner being. At the same time, they tend to look at other persons in terms only of their importance and usefulness. Despite the cool and competent persona, Threes endure plenty of psychic strain as they cover up their real selves, keeping others (and themselves) at a distance from their inner doubts and weaknesses. In this, they deceive first themselves, then others.

When Threes disintegrate, they experience a growing frustration with failure and may turn hostile. They follow the arrow to the Nine and, like an unhealthy Nine, no longer see life as worth the effort. They no longer feel guilty over their hostile actions and words; they tune out their feelings. Failure, and their inability to face what it might mean, provokes a malicious reaction. The energetic, competent and efficient aspects that define so much of what is good in them are lost.

When Threes integrate by moving against the arrow, they take on the best qualities of the Six. Threes tend to rank personal success as priority number one, and often use others as the means to their ends. Not so the Six, who is loyal to the group and faithful in relationships. By integrating in this direction, Threes become cooperative and concerned with the welfare of others. Also, they become more attuned to their conscience. Growing awareness of an inner self develops. They realize their own weaknesses and their need for "something more" (this being the grace of God) than their own competence. The Three begins to cultivate and care for others for their own sake, no longer as means to an egocentric end. Best of all, Threes reach a point where they are, quite simply, honest... even when no one is looking.

The Four is "an artist of life," bringing to the canvas of everyday existence a sensibility that is *not* "everyday." To the Four, the past—romantic and distant—and the future—filled with projects that may or may not materialize—bear the most significance, not the moment at hand. The Four, in addition to flights of imagination backwards and forwards, engages in a sophisticated presentation of the self, esteeming the self as special, as "finer" than others. Fours are actors, not only in their scene-setting but in their sensitivity and emotional richness. They are subject to variable feelings that buffet them across a spectrum of moods, from depression to elation. Unwilling to join the human race in its often pedestrian pursuits, they can find themselves isolated, unfulfilled and unaccomplished—despite considerable talent and promise—and feeling defective and depressed.

When they disintegrate, Fours follow the arrow to Two. There they become dependent, cleaving to others for support. They develop a need for the other—the other as caregiver. Like Twos, dependent Fours find their self-worth in being appreciated by others. They become aware that they have let the years roll by, that their dreams have not been realized. Like an unhealthy Two, they spiral out of control emotionally, overwhelmed by negative feelings.

By moving against the arrow, Fours take on the healthy characteristics of the One. They learn to discipline themselves, to press themselves upon the environment. They learn to take themselves "in hand," to reason with themselves, to move into action. They seek achievement and become aware of objective values. No longer helplessly pushed and pulled by their feelings, they put their gifts to work in practical ways. They move beyond introversion and subjectivity yet, once in action, express the richness of their interiority. They become special in the healthy sense of that word.

To the Five, "to know is to be." Fives are natural ascetics, contemplatives and gnostics. Their "real" world is in their mind, thus they are detached, private, interior beings. They fear envelopment by the world and by others; they fear losing their identity, they fear giving up a part of themselves in order to give to others. They hoard their time, emotions, thoughts and possessions as means to preserve their safety and autonomy against a threatening environment.

Deteriorating Fives, as they turn ever more inward, follow the arrow to Seven, where they become impulsive and irrational. Like Sevens, unhealthy Fives avoid the unpleasant aspects of life, allowing fantasies and distorted thoughts to take hold. They detach from any practical application of their mental gifts. This development is coupled with restless action (another characteristic of the Seven). Paranoia and isolation set in and fear becomes an ever present reality.

When they integrate, Fives move against the arrow to Eight. Eights instinctively press themselves against the world, modeling an assertiveness the Five needs. Fives, by learning to channel their turblent minds in creative ways, discharge their thoughts in purposive action, putting into practice their great store of theory and abstraction. They learn to act. Even if they do not know everything about the subject at hand, they become ready to stand up and be counted in the world of action. As a result, fear diminishes.

Sixes, compliant, ambivalent, overly serious, are both fearful and aware of their fears. They perceive the world as hostile, requiring barriers of psychic protection. They shy away from new ideas, preferring the tried and true, the proven path, the tradition that can be counted on in a world of ebb and flow. Unable to trust themselves, they look to the church, the firm, the party or some other authority to give them the assurance they need. Frightened and tentative on their own, they can brim with confidence when they know their cause is sanctioned by authority. Generally phobic, they can become counterphobic as well, defying the fears that prey upon them.

Unhealthy Sixes follow the arrow to Three, where they become hyperactive, aggressive and insecure, ruthlessly seeking their ends with bluster and intimidation. In defying their fears and ambivalences, they pursue success at any cost. They can become violent in an attempt to conceal their fears and inferiorities. They may act out against those whom they believe have persecuted them.

The Six makes peace with his or her self by moving against the arrow into the space of the self-accepting Nine. There, inner conflicts ease and reconciliation of contradictory impulses becomes possible. Peace and harmony become important values. Sixes become less anxious about what the group thinks. At the same time, they become more trusting of divine intentions. They learn to "die" in order to "live," countering their ingrained predispositions with Christian wisdom. Even in the absence of guaranteed security, they venture into the unknown. They become inwardly stable, less fearful, more trusting of others.

Sevens, optimistic seekers of perpetual joy, tend to avert their gaze when trials and unpleasant truths come their way. They follow the false gospel of bliss, living amidst a whirl of pleasures, multiple options and frivolous entertainments. In this, they are like spoiled children, demanding instant gratification, overindulging the senses and taking little responsibility towards the unhappier aspects of life. On the plus side, they are likeable and sometimes irresistible. They are quick learners, jovial companions and engaging conversationalists. Yet deep in the psyche is a nagging dread of meaninglessness and extinction, of an end to the never ending party. As a result, they run faster and faster through life, afraid to look back, afraid a menacing reality will catch them if they stop to catch their breath.

Sevens disintegrate along the path to One, moving with the arrow to introduce into their manic selves a semblance of order. In doing this they become, like unhealthy Ones, aggressive and punitive. They resent having lost, through excess and unreal expectations, the hope of a trouble-free life. The pseudo-discipline resulting from the move to One is too little, too late. They resent the limits they impose on themselves and rebel, leading to even more outrageous behavior, continuing deterioration and possible physical violence.

Sevens balance their lives with a move to Five. Working against the arrow, they slow down a bit. They become more observant. Awareness of the Transcendent grows. ("Be still and know that I am God"). They learn to avail themselves of reason and moderation. They learn that the trials of living are a means of growing in the spiritual life, and that "Whom the Lord loveth he chasteneth." Holiness becomes more important than superficial happiness. And they realize that trials are "only for a season." By looking at the world in depth, they savor the pleasures of life more fully and with greater gratitude.

Eights are "bigger than the world," instinctive and powerful, natural leaders. They are choleric, energetic, intimidating, characterized by all or nothing thinking. They exercise control and play power games. They dismiss the authority of others, be that authority political, legal, moral or medical. While uncanny at ferreting out the weaknesses of others, they are cunning in hiding their own. ("Never let the other guy see you sweat"). Despite their lust for domination, Eights also seek to set right the injustices of the world, carrying within them a soft spot for the truly weak and downtrodden. They like to play the role of tribune for the oppressed.

Eights, when they follow the arrow to Five, enter a realm in which they fear for survival. The people upon whom they have trampled are now potential aggressors, ready to strike the person who has dominated them. Therefore they become paranoid, like an unhealthy Five. Eights in this state withdraw from the world of action and, like a Five, watch from a distance. They are defined by suspicion, delusion, isolation and vulnerability to total defeat.

When Eights move against the arrow to reach the Two, they place their instinctive energy on the side of good. Eights, already drawn to the underdog in their healthier moments, now move in a more principled manner to come to the aid of those in need. Their natural aggressiveness is tempered by empathy for the needs and feelings of others. In addition, they "open up" and let others see beneath the armored exterior, allowing a glimpse of vulnerability. To show honest emotion is a risk to them but, also, a path to the truly human.

Nines seek unity and tranquility, an aspiration that too often leads to passivity and drifting. They excel at peacemaking when healthy but slip into indifference and neglect when unhealthy. They fail to order and discipline their lives, to set clear goals and valid tasks. Progress in self-development is slow and spotty, hampered by a smothering inertia. They are prone to regress, to slide back to homeostasis. Their personalities can become bland and blank. They are "neither hot nor cold." Afraid to set painful but necessary priorities, they tread the backwaters of life... and the strong, main currents of life pass them by.

Nines disintegrate by following the arrow to Six. Having reached a state of despair over their lack of accomplishment, they are beset by anxiety, like a fearful Six. Normally placid Nines become angry and strike out, even as they remain dependent on others. They become self-punishing and find themselves filled with doubts about their course in life. They doubt the good intentions of others, too, reacting like an angry and defensive Six—sometimes with violence—towards anyone who seeks to nudge them into action.

The integrating Nine moves against the arrow by taking on the healthy qualities of the Three. Nines at this point become more assertive, exchanging their tendency to withdraw in favor of action in the world. They learn to set goals, to aspire after achievement. They develop a sense of self-worth; healthy emotions break through their placid exterior. They stop being cyphers. They are able to take charge of their lives and develop independence and confidence, secure in the knowledge that their quest for unity will find its place in the overarching providence of God.

Ones seek order, decency, a clear conscience. They see the world as black and white; they despise ambiguity. Above all, they seek *rectitude*; they strive to be right about things large and small. They are good and dutiful people, interested in fair play and proper conduct. Yet the harder they try to be good, the more active the devils become, pricking their conscience with obsessive remorse. They come to view life as a series of tasks that can never be fully accomplished. Like Sisyphus, they reach the top of the mountain only to see the rock roll back down the slope. They can never reach the goal, complete the chore or master the challenge in keeping with the standards they have set. In their view, the good is *always* the enemy of the best. For being finite and imperfect—for being, in a word, human—they judge themselves severely.

When Ones follow the arrow to Four, they collapse beneath self-imposed burdens. They become depressed, suffering dramatically like a melancholy Four. The "perfect" has eluded them and they give up, sinking into anger and dispair. They feel guilty about their shortcomings and upset about the narrow-minded state into which they have sunk, yet they cannot rescue themselves. Their hypocrisies become ever more apparent even as they condemn others with self-righteous zeal.

Ones find balance by integrating to the Seven. At Seven, they find optimism, a sense of fun, a break with routine. Ones at Seven take life and themselves less seriously. By integrating as they do, they stop resenting the world and its imperfections. They strive less but achieve more. They learn that virtue is its own reward and brood less on the peccadilloes of others. They also become valued for the guidance they can give, becoming figures of wisdom. Indeed, they become "wise as serpents but gentle as doves."

All of the types need to stop short-circuiting their personalities within the narrow confines of their egos and, instead, to open their inner selves to God. They need to dislodge the self-centered self, to clear away the blocks and blinders. They need to clean the smudges from the glass and let the Spirit shine in. In short, they need to open the inner spaces of the psyche, to de-solidify the constricted soul, to manifest their rebirth in daily living. They need to allow the new image in the old psyche to "give birth" to fuller life; they need to become by the power of the Holy Spirit, in the words of Jacob Boehme, like "a branch pulled from its own essence, becoming green in the spirit of Christ."[125]

---

[125]Antoine Faivre, *Theosophy, Imagination, Tradition, Studies in Western Esotericism*, p. 143

19

Gnosis and Integration

"The soul must have a complete alphabet."
—Søren Kierkegaard

The art of spiritual living involves taking one's self in hand, refusing to be passive in the face of habitual sins and failings, and moving ahead with the business of sanctification. This requires perspective, objectivity and (according to St. Paul) a "sober view" of one's self. In the words of a shrewd student of personality, "You have to address yourself, preach to yourself, question yourself. You must say to your soul: 'Why art thou cast down'—what business have you to be disquieted? You must turn on yourself, upbraid yourself, condemn yourself, exhort yourself, and say to yourself: 'Hope thou in God'"[126]

To find the incentive to embark on spiritual work, one needs to have a sense of longing, a sense of incompleteness... a sense of sin. "It is not the healthy who need a doctor, but the sick" (Matthew 9:12). One must know what it is to suffer (emotionally, mentally or physically), to feel need, to have a true "conviction of sin." We are, as scripture teaches, sinners born and bred. "We all like sheep have gone astray, each of us has turned to his own way" (Isaiah 53:6). And in the words of St. Paul, "All have sinned and fall short of the glory of God" (Romans 3:23).

---

[126] D. Martyn Lloyd-Jones, *Spiritual Depression*, p. 21

Everyone sins in the sense of breaking some (or, in some cases, most!) of the commandments (idolatry, coveting, lying, theft, adultery etc.). Here, however, we do not speak of specific sins but of sin as a substantive condition of alienation, of alienation from the Divine. It is the condition inherent in a fallen race. It is the condition out of which the visible sins arise. It is the condition in which sin occupies the essence of every fallen creature. Thus it is the human essence, the spirit, that has to be cleansed and reactivated first, that has to be "born again" of the Holy Spirit, after which it is able to flow forth into a soul (mind, heart and will) that is increasingly in harmony and balance with itself, that is learning to be at peace with itself. By these means, the Spirit of God is able to absorb into its own purposes more and more of the personality of the believer, thereby freeing that believer from the fetters of self and liberating him or her for proper and joyful service.

To these ends, men and women of all Enneagram types need to abandon the strategies of self-salvation. They need instead to open themselves to the Holy Spirit. Specifically:

- The Two needs to turn from compulsive service and self-sacrifice to the idea of grace, to an acceptance of God's gifts, to joy and peace in the undeserved merit that God confers.

- The Three needs to turn from competitive striving for self-defined fame and fortune to an understanding of God's will, to a realization that one's skills need to find their place in the Creator's plans.

- The Four needs to move from a yearning for uniqueness and self-styled authenticity to a life that seeks union with God, wherein true "specialness" finds its fulfillment.

- The Five needs to turn from obsessive acquisition of knowledge to a sense of God's providence, to a realization that God may be trusted to provide abundantly for all of life's needs.

- The Six needs to shift from anxiety over personal security to a life in which God is trusted to provide all necessary authority, all proper assurance, over and above the rules and regulations of lesser entities.

- The Seven needs to move from a world of titillating experiences and avoidance of serious matters to a life in which God is honored through necessary suffering and sacrifice.

- The Eight needs to move from the worldly exercise of autonomy and domination to a life in relationship to God and filled with compassion and service to others.

- The Nine must shift from indolence and aimlessness to an understanding that he or she is accepted by God and asked by Him to do good work and good works, with purpose and dedication.

- The One needs to stop judging the world on its lack of perfection and realize that God calls him or her to participate in the *process* of redemption; to accept a nurtured, organic fulfillment in God's time.

The regeneration, the "rebirth," of fallen humanity begins with God's act of grace towards men and women, with his decision to grant favor on the basis of the cross. By means of the work accomplished on Calvary, He implants his Spirit in the human spirit. Thus begins the "Great Work" of sanctification, the transforming and transmuting work of the divine in the human. It is a work that is, in the words of Antoine Faivre (after the mystic Angelus Silesius), a "transmutation through the only immortal tincture, Jesus Christ crucified."[127]

In response to the divine initiative, the human subject is drawn into Christ. "I am the good shepherd; I know my sheep and my sheep know me" (John 10:14). In this supernatural bond, man's fallen spirit is enlivened. He becomes a "new man." Worldly wisdom, affections and desires are replaced by the "folly" of the cross. Once proud but now humbled, man learns to depend on God to save him by grace, in the Spirit. Thus in *justification*, man is "born again" and the Christian walk begins; in *sanctification*, the walk becomes the drama and the focus of Christian living.

---

[127] *Theosophy, Imagination, Tradition, Studies in Western Esotericism*, p. 72

In the final analysis, one "lives" the Enneagram as a form of knowledge, as a mode of thought, as a *gnosis*. The Enneagram is not, it turns out, a striving after personality integration so much as it is an active, aware "knowing" that serves to transform and liberate the "knower." Slowly, imperceptibly, by the use of attention, reflection and perseverance, it leads to change. It lights a flame of quiet joy to illumine the interior life. One is able at last to live "whole," in peace, simultaneously justified and a sinner (in Luther's phrase), alert to grace and filled with gratitude.

The Enneagram is a means to understanding and healing the soul. It is a form of knowledge, complex, detailed and accurate. It aims to balance mind, emotions and will. There will come a time, however, when the Enneagram can be left behind, along with other forms of psychological wisdom. Even as Thomas Aquinas left behind his incomparable *Summa*, considering it so much "straw" in the aftermath of his mystical vision, so too one day will the adept of the Enneagram leave behind his means and method, his dynamics of integration and disintegration, his types and triads. At that point he will be released into a higher realm, a fuller vision, a happier state. Transcendence will be realized at last... if not in this life, in a better one to come.

Afterword

*"It is fitting that Christ's body was resurrected with its
scars so that he may present eternally to his Father, in
prayers that he addresses to him for us,
what death he suffered for men."*
—St. Thomas Aquinas

Thomas "the doubter," of whom we spoke earlier, refused at first to believe in the risen Jesus. "Unless I see the nail marks in his hands and put my finger where the nails were, and put my hand into his side, I will not believe it" (John 20:25).

One can sympathize with Thomas. We, too, would wish to see proof of the stupendous claim being made. "Raised from the dead? Show me."

Interestingly, Thomas asked to see Jesus' *wounds*. He did not ask to see Jesus as such but to see the *wounds* of Jesus' humiliation.

How did Thomas know there would *be* wounds? One could easily imagine the risen Christ as healed and spotless in his glory, even as he had appeared to Peter, James and John at his Transfiguration. But Thomas *knew* of the wounds, and it was these he wished to see—and touch.

Jesus himself, it would appear, had introduced the subject. It was he, the Sunday before, who showed the disciples his wounds when he first appeared to them in his resurrected state. ("He showed them his hands and side"—John 20:20). Upon seeing Jesus and his wounds, the disciples appear—surprisingly—to have been released from the

157

grief and fear that had paralyzed them. ("The disciples were overjoyed when they saw the Lord"—v. 20). They do not appear to have been saddened by the sight of the wounds, nor to have been repelled by visible reminders of the Saviour's agony and death. Rather, the sight appears to have effected their healing.

Thomas, for his part, demanded proof of the resurrection for himself. He sought tangible evidence of the marks of suffering and death. Jesus granted his wish. As a result, the "doubter" was healed, and set right with Jesus. ("My Lord and my God" v. 28).

The Resurrection, unaccompanied by the all-important wounds, would have distanced Jesus from his followers. It would have diminished the sense of his humanness. He had, after all, shared himself with his disciples fully; he had shared himself even unto death. Now, resurrected, yet still bearing his wounds, he would continue to share in their humanness even as he interceded for them. The marks of his death would testify to this sharing. The marks would prove that his death—as well as his resurrection and his intercession- was incontestably *real*.

This was vital. The events of the previous days had left the disciples shattered, aimless, grief-stricken. By appearing in *his* woundedness, Jesus expressed solidarity with *their* woundedness. His glorified body, which would carry forever the wounds inflicted in death, even as he interceded eternally for his people, was a sign that the love of God transcends the marks of suffering.

All persons bear within themselves a cluster of interior wounds, of psychic insults, inflicted at various stages of the life journey. The Enneagram explores the outworking of these wounds in the form of the capital sins: pride, deceit and envy, greed, fear and gluttony, lust, sloth and anger. It probes deeply into the complexes and compulsions, the sins and slaveries, that thrive beneath the surface of the unredeemed self. It provides a vital perspective on this self, it cautions against its wiles, and it points to liberation.

With the help of the Enneagram, one may experience healing of one's wounded nature, even as the scars remain; one may experience integration, even as the fault lines of potential disintegration remain.

The Enneagram does not allow one to forget his or her darker side. The humility thus engendered, the continuing awareness of one's indwelling sins and shortcomings, keeps psychic inflation in check.

Even as the glorified Jesus bore the wounds of his suffering, so the Spirit-healed believer bears the marks of his or her pain and humiliation as well. Yet, as in the case of the risen Jesus, the wounded nature is transcended. The Holy Spirit, working in the human spirit and flowing into the human psyche, heals the deepest wounds. Yet the wounds remain tangible, sometimes even visible, as did the lame hip of Jacob after he wrestled at the Jabbok.

One's wounds are an integral part of the self. They have a purpose only they can serve. They are, in fact, signs of one's "providential disequilibrium" (Frithjof Schuon). Objective awareness of this disequilibrium—and of the providential means by which God works through it to restore the soul to balance—*this* is the sum of wisdom. God balances the scales; He provides the one thing needed. In weakness, He gives strength; in loss, gain.

Human beings are created in the image of God. Though fallen from a once noble estate, there remains to them the promise of redemption and return, of the deliverance of spirit, soul and body, of an eternal inheritance to those who are called according to the purposes of God. Faith is asked ("blessed are those who have not seen and yet have believed"—John. 20:29) and from faith, the fruit of good works.

Bibliography

Adler, Gerhard, and Aniela Jaffé, *C. G. Jung: Letters* (Princeton University Press, 1975).

Barth, Karl, *Church Dogmatics, A Selection*, selected by Helmut Gollwitzer, translated by G. W. Bromiley, (Westminster John Knox Press, Louisville, Ky.,1994).

Boehme, Jacob, *The Forty Questions of the Soul* and *The Clavis*, translated by John Sparrow (Sure Fire Press [An Imprint of the Holmes Publishing Group], Edmonds, Wash.,1993).

Bonhoeffer, Dietrich, *The Cost of Discipleship* (MacMillan Publishing Co., Inc., New York, 1963).

Bonner, Anthony, and Eve Bonner, *Doctor Illuminatus: A Ramon Llull Reader* (Princeton University Press, 1993).

Borella, Jean, "René Guénon and the Traditionalist School," from *Modern Esoteric Spirituality,* edited by Antoine Faivre and Jacob Needleman; associate editor, Karen Voss (The Crossroad Publishing Company, New York, 1995).

Bridges, Jerry, *The Pursuit of Holiness* (NavPress, Colorado Springs, 1989).

Browne, Sir Thomas, *Religio Medici, Letter to a Friend* and *Christian Morals,* edited by W. A. Greenhill (Sherwood, Sugden & Company Publishers, Peru, Ill., 1990).

Bullinger, E. W., *Number in Scripture* (Kregel Publications, Grand Rapids, Mich., 1967).

Burckhardt, Titus, *Alchemy: Science of the Cosmos, Science of the Soul,* translated by William Stoddart (Fons Vitae, Louisville, Ky., 1997).

Calvin, John, *Institutes of the Christian Religion*, translated by Henry Beveridge (William B. Eerdmans Publishing Company, Grand Rapids, Mich.,1997).

Carnell, Corbin Scott, *Bright Shadow of Reality: C. S. Lewis and the Feeling Intellect* (Eerdmans, 1974).

Chesterton, G. K., *Orthodoxy* (Image Books, Garden City, N. Y., 1959).

Cohen, Edmund D., *C. G. Jung and the Scientific Attitude* (Philosophical Library, New York, 1975).

Dillenberger, John, *Martin Luther: Selections from His Writings* (Anchor Books Doubleday, New York, 1961).

Faivre, Antoine, *Access to Western Esotericism* (State University of New York Press, Albany, N. Y., 1994).

———, *Theosophy, Imagination, Tradition: Studies in Western Esotericism*, translated by Christine Rhone (State University of New York Press, 2000).

Fénelon, Francois de Salignac de La Mothe, *Let Go, To Get Peace and Real Joy,* based on the translation by Mildred Whitney Stillman (Whitaker House, Springdale, Penn., 1973).

Franz, Marie-Louise von, *Alchemical Active Imagination* (Shambhala, Boston, Mass., 1997).

Guénon, René, *Fundamental Symbols: The Universal Language of Sacred Science,* translated by Alvin Moore Jr. (Quinta Essentia, Cambridge, UK, 1995).

Guthrie, Donald, and J. A. Motyer, editors, *The New Bible Commentary* (Eerdmans, 1991).

Hallesby, Ole, *Temperament and the Christian Faith* (Augsburg Publishing House, Minneapolis, 1962).

Horney, Karen, *Neurosis and Human Growth: The Struggle Toward Self-Realization* (W. W. Norton and Company, Inc., New York, 1991).

Huxley, Aldous, *The Perennial Philosophy* (Harper & Row Publishers, Inc., New York, 1944).

James, William, *The Varieties of Religious Experience* (Penguin Books, New York, 1986).

Jung, Carl Gustav, *Psychological Types* (Princeton University Press, Princeton, N. J., 1971).

Kant, Immanuel, *Anthropology from a Pragmatic Point of View* translated by Victor Lyle Dowdell (Southern Illinois University Press, Carbondale and Edwardsville, Ill., 1996).

Kaufmann, Walter, *Without Guilt and Justice: From Decidophobia to Autonomy* (Dell Publishing Co., Inc., New York, 1973).

LaHaye, Tim, *Transformed Temperaments* (Living Books, Tyndale, 1993).

Lewis, C. S., *The Abolition of Man*, (Macmillan, 1969).

———, *The Discarded Image: An Introduction to Medieval and Renaissance Literature* (Cambridge University Press, UK, 1998).

———, *George MacDonald, An Anthology* (Macmillan, 1947).

———, *Letters to Malcolm: Chiefly on Prayer* (Harcourt Brace Jovanovich, New York and London).

———, *Mere Christianity* (Macmillan, 1976).

Lloyd-Jones, D. Martyn, *Spiritual Depression: Its Causes and Its Cure* (Eerdmans, 1982).

Lubac, Henri De, *Theology in History* (Ignatius Press, San Franciso, 1996).

Machen, J. Gresham, *What is Faith?* (The Banner of Truth Trust, Edinburgh, 1991).

Maistre, Joseph de, *The Works of Joseph de Maistre*, translated by Jack Lively (Macmillan, 1965).

Moore, James, *Gurdjieff: A Biography* (Element Books Inc., Boston, 1999).

Mullens, E. Y., *The Axioms of Religion* (The Judson Press, Philadelphia, 1908).

Naranjo, Claudio, *Character and Neurosis: An Integrative View* (Gateways/IDHHB, Inc., Nevada City, Cal., 1994).

————, *Ennea-Type Structures: Self-Analysis for the Seeker* (Gateways/IDHHB, 1990).

Nee, Watchman, *The Spiritual Man* (Christian Fellowship Publishers, Inc., New York, 1977).

The New Encyclopaedia Britannica, Vol 9, *Micropaedia* (Chicago, 1998).

Oldham, John M., and Lois B. Morris, *Personality Self-Portrait: Why You Think, Work, Love and Act the Way You Do* (Bantam Books, New York, 1991).

Packer, J. I., *Concise Theology: A Guide to Historic Christian Beliefs* (Tyndale House Publishers, Inc., Wheaton, Ill., 1993).

————, *God's Words: Studies of Key Bible Themes* (InterVarsity Press, Downers Grove, Ill., 1981).

————, *"Fundamentalism" and the Word of God* (Eerdmans, 1977).

————, *I Want to Be a Christian* (Tyndale, 1977).

————, *Knowing God* (InterVarsity Press, Downers Grove, Ill., 1973).

————, and Carolyn Nystrom, *Never Beyond Hope: How God Touches & Uses Imperfect People* (Intervarsity, 2000).

————, *Rediscovering Holiness* (Servant Publications, Ann Arbor, Mich., 1992).

Raffel, Burton, *The Annotated Milton* (Bantam Books, New York, 1999).

Riso, Don Richard, with Russ Hudson, *Personality Types, Using the Enneagram for Self-Discovery* (Houghton Mifflin Co., Boston, New York, 1996).

Rohr, Richard, and Andreas Ebert, *Discovering the Enneagram: An Ancient Tool for a New Spiritual Journey* (The Crossroad Publishing Company, New York,1992).

Ryle, J. C., *Holiness* (Evangelical Press, Darlington, England, 1999).

Schuon, Frithjof, *Survey of Metaphysics and Esoterism*, translated by Gustavo Polit (World Wisdom Books, Bloomington, Ind., 1986).

Stafford, William S., *Disordered Loves: Healing the Seven Deadly Sins* (Cowley Publications, Boston, Mass., 1994).

Versluis, Arthur, *Song of the Cosmos: An Introduction to Traditional Cosmology* (PRISM PRESS, Dorset, 1991).

Vollmar, Klausbernd, *The Secret of Enneagrams: Mapping the Personality* (Element Books, Rockport, Mass., 1997).

Warfield, Benjamin B., *Faith and Life* (The Banner of Truth Trust, 1990).

Index

T

Tauler 122
Teresa of Avila 122
Tersteegan 122

V

van Wulfen, Willem 66
Versluis, Arthur 10, 164
Vollmar, Klausbernd 5, 164
von Franz, Marie-Louise 7, 8, 10,
    161

W

Warfield, Benjamin B. 34, 164
Watts, Isaac 26
Whyte, Alexander 59, 79, 83
Wilde, Oscar 25
William of St. Thierry 122

BOOK ORDER FORM
Dimensions of the Enneagram

Name: _____

Address: _____

City: _____ State:_____ Zip:_____

Phone: _____ Fax: _____

E-mail: _____

Mail to Name: _____

Address: _____

City: _____ State: _____ Zip:_____

	Quantity	Cost/Book	Total
DIMENSIONS OF THE ENNEAGRAM		$16.95	
Shipping			
6% MI Tax			
Total			

Shipping charges: $4.00 for one book, $2.00 for each additional book

Please mail this form with check or money order to:
The Lion and The Bee
P.O. Box 504
Marshall, MI 49068

Author Tom Isham is also available to speak with groups and give workshops on the Enneagram. For more information, please contact him at the above address or by e-mailing Aisham735@aol.com.